CAMPAIGN 388

NAVAL BATTLE OF CRETE 1941

The Royal Navy at Breaking Point

ANGUS KONSTAM

ILLUSTRATED BY ADAM TOOBY
Series editor Nikolai Bogdanovic

OSPREY PUBLISHING
Bloomsbury Publishing Plc
Kemp House, Chawley Park, Cumnor Hill, Oxford OX2 9PH, UK
29 Earlsfort Terrace, Dublin 2, Ireland
1385 Broadway, 5th Floor, New York, NY 10018, USA
E-mail: info@ospreypublishing.com
www.ospreypublishing.com

OSPREY is a trademark of Osprey Publishing Ltd

First published in Great Britain in 2023

© Osprey Publishing Ltd, 2023

A catalogue record for this book is available from the British Library.

ISBN: PB 9781472854049; eBook 9781472854032; ePDF 9781472854025;
XML 9781472854018

23 24 25 26 27   10 9 8 7 6 5 4 3 2 1

Maps by Bounford.com
3D BEVs by Paul Kime
Index by Fionbar Lyons
Typeset by PDQ Digital Media Solutions, Bungay, UK
Printed and bound in India by Replika Press Private Ltd.

Artist's note

Readers can find out more about the work of battlescene illustrator Adam Tooby at the following website:

www.adamtooby.com

Osprey Publishing supports the Woodland Trust, the UK's leading woodland conservation charity.

To find out more about our authors and books visit **www.ospreypublishing.com**. Here you will find extracts, author interviews, details of forthcoming events and the option to sign up for our newsletter.

Acronyms and abbreviations

AA	anti-aircraft
GOC	General Officer Commanding
HACS	High-Angle Control System
JG	Jadgeschwader
KG	Kampfgeschwader
LG	Lehrgeschwader
MAS	Motoscafo Armato Silurante (torpedo-armed motorboat)
MNBDO	Mobile Naval Base Defence Organization
nm	nautical miles
RAN	Royal Australian Navy
RN	Royal Navy
StG	Sturzkampfgeschwader
ZG	Zerstörergeschwader

A note on measure

Both Imperial and metric measurements have been used in this book. A conversion table is provided below:
1in. = 2.54cm
1ft = 0.3m
1 yard = 0.9m
1 mile = 1.6km
1 nautical mile = 1.85km
1lb = 0.45kg
1 long ton = 1.02 metric tonnes

1mm = 0.039in.
1cm= 0.39in.
1m = 1.09 yards
1km = 0.62 miles
1kg = 2.2lb
1 metric tonne = 0.98 long tons

Photographs

Unless otherwise indicated, all the photographic images that appear in this work are from the Stratford Archive.

Front cover (main image): RN Force B under attack in the Kasos Strait, 29 May 1941. (Adam Tooby)
Title page photograph: The RN Mediterranean Fleet's battle squadron consisted of four Queen Elizabeth-class battleships. Here, *Valiant*, *Queen Elizabeth* and *Barham* are pictured from the deck of the fourth ship in the line, *Warspite*.

Key to military symbols

××××× Army Group	×××× Army	××× Corps	×× Division	× Brigade	III Regiment	II Battalion
I Company/Battery	••• Platoon	•• Section	• Squad	Infantry	Artillery	Cavalry
Airborne	Unit HQ	Air defence	Air Force	Air mobile	Air transportable	Amphibious
Anti-tank	Armour	Air aviation	Bridging	Engineer	Headquarters	Maintenance
Medical	Missile	Mountain	Navy	Nuclear, biological, chemical	Ordnance	Parachute
Reconnaissance	Signal	Supply	Transport movement	Rocket artillery	Air defence artillery	

Key to unit identification

Unit identifier — Parent unit
Commander
(+) with added elements
(−) less elements

CONTENTS

INTRODUCTION   5
Origins of the campaign

CHRONOLOGY   11

OPPOSING COMMANDERS   13
Allied . Axis

OPPOSING FORCES   17
Allied . Allied order of battle . Axis . Axis order of battle

OPPOSING PLANS   25
Allied . Axis

THE CAMPAIGN   29
The prelude . The fleet deploys . The invasion . The first clashes . The Luftwaffe strikes
Black Thursday . Mountbatten's sortie . Keeping up the pressure . The evacuation

AFTERMATH   90

THE BATTLEFIELD TODAY   93

FURTHER READING   94

INDEX   95

The strategic situation, April–June 1941

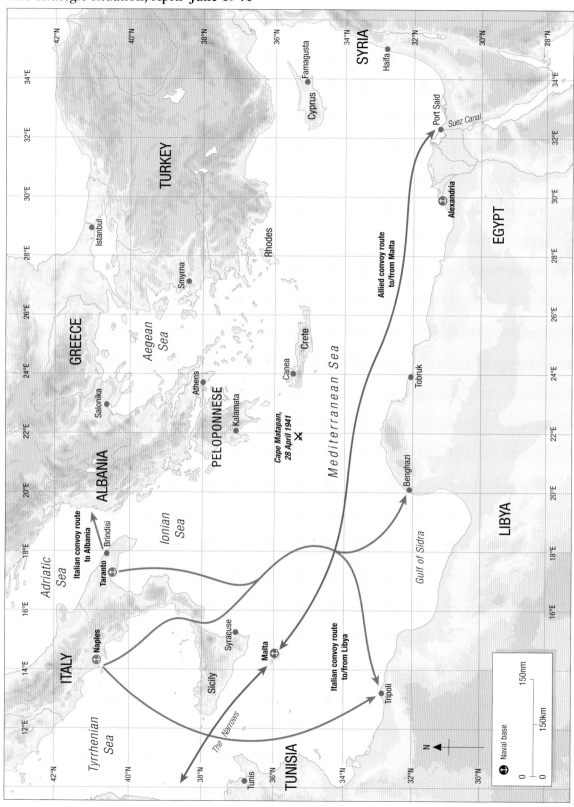

INTRODUCTION

In March 1941, the tide of war in the Mediterranean seemed to be flowing Britain's way. The Italians had been driven out of Cyrenaica in the Western Desert, and the situation seemed so stable that Prime Minister Winston Churchill decided to send British and Commonwealth troops to Greece, which was being half-heartedly attacked by the Italians. On 28 March, Admiral Andrew Cunningham's Mediterranean Fleet inflicted a major defeat on the Italian Regia Marina off Cape Matapan. Effectively, this secured Britain's control over the eastern Mediterranean. The tide, though, was about to turn. Throughout that month the Germans had been building up their strength in Libya and the Balkans. Two days after Matapan, Rommel made his move, and within two weeks had driven the British Army out of Libya. A week later, on 6 April, the German blitzkrieg began in the Balkans. Yugoslavia fell within days, and by mid-April the Greeks and their Commonwealth allies were in full retreat. This change of fortune had been as rapid as it was dramatic.

The Allies had been singularly unprepared for this two-pronged onslaught, and so were outmatched and outfought. Key to this German success was air power. With over a thousand aircraft at its disposal the Luftwaffe also enjoyed complete air superiority over its opponents. The rapid German advance also meant that there was now a real danger that the 60,000 Commonwealth troops in Greece would be lost. So, on 22 April, Cunningham was ordered to evacuate these men by whatever means he could. This marked the beginning of what would become one of the Royal Navy's most gruelling and costly campaigns of the entire war.

Cunningham was well aware that, having overrun Greece, the Germans were preparing to invade Crete. This invasion would probably come by both air and sea, with the Luftwaffe supporting the assault, and protecting the invaders. Opposing them would be the small Commonwealth garrison on the island, reinforced by troops evacuated from Greece, and supported by a handful of understrength RAF squadrons. Protecting the island from

Admiral Andrew B. Cunningham, Commander-in-Chief of the British Mediterranean Fleet, was arguably one of the best naval commanders of the war. Even he, though, for all his skills, had nothing to counter the Luftwaffe's air superiority in the campaign apart from his own determination.

invasion by sea was the job of the Royal Navy, regardless of the deadly threat posed by the Luftwaffe.

What followed has been described as one of the darkest periods in the Royal Navy's history. On 20 May, the leading elements of a German parachute corps landed on Crete, and gained a foothold on the island. Royal Naval warships successfully intercepted and destroyed two invasion convoys, but these victories came at a price. The warships were subjected to heavy, relentless air attacks. In the space of two days, two cruisers and four destroyers were sunk while two irreplaceable battleships and a carrier were badly damaged. More, though, was to come. Protected by the Luftwaffe the German toehold on Crete was reinforced from the air, and the military situation deteriorated rapidly. Cunningham was duly ordered to evacuate the troops.

Over the next four days, 16,500 grateful soldiers were evacuated in the face of relentless air attacks. The ships and men were pushed to the very limits of their endurance, and a further cruiser and two destroyers were sunk. Several other British or Australian warships were so badly damaged they barely made it back to Alexandria. By 1 June, though, the costly evacuation drew to a close as the Germans overran the evacuation beaches. Back in Alexandria, the battered Mediterranean Fleet licked its wounds, and prepared for a fresh round of air attacks. This assault, though, never came, thanks to the diversion of the Luftwaffe to support the Axis invasion of the Soviet Union. So, the Mediterranean Fleet lived to fight another day.

It was a bloody chapter in the Royal Navy's history, but it was also an inspiring one. Without the Mediterranean Fleet, tens of thousands of Allied troops would have been sacrificed in Greece and Crete. At one stage, as losses mounted, Cunningham faced pressure from the Admiralty to withdraw. He replied, 'It takes the Navy three years to build a ship. It will take three hundred years to build a new tradition. The evacuation will continue.' This came to symbolize the Navy's determination as Cunningham put it; 'to not let the Army down'. It was an attitude that would serve the Navy well during the battles that lay ahead.

ORIGINS OF THE CAMPAIGN

On 10 June 1940, with German tanks just 30 miles from Paris, Italy declared war on France. The Italian leader Benito Mussolini was determined to share the fruits of victory. He also declared war on France's ally Great Britain, which meant that the Regia Marina (the Italian Royal Navy) would immediately be thrust into a struggle to the death with the British Royal Navy's powerful Mediterranean Fleet. The following day, the Regia Aeronautica (Italian Air Force) carried out the first of hundreds of bombing raids on Malta, the home of the British Mediterranean Fleet. By then, though, the fleet's commander Admiral Cunningham had already moved it eastwards, to his secondary naval base at Alexandria in Egypt. The course of the hard-fought naval struggle that followed would be dominated by these two British bases, and by a third, Gibraltar, at the western end of the Mediterranean Sea.

In peacetime, the role of the Mediterranean Fleet was to safeguard the sea route that stretched from Port Said on the Suez Canal in the east to Gibraltar in the west – a distance of 1,900nm. The fortress island of Malta

The Leander-class light cruiser *Ajax*, pictured alongside at Piraeus, the port serving Athens, during the Greek campaign. She was also involved in the subsequent evacuation, and went on to play a prominent part in the Crete campaign.

lay midway between the two points. In theory, Cunningham's job was to protect this strategically vital sea route. In practice, though, this would be almost impossible, as the Regia Marina, backed up by the Regia Aeronautica, dominated the waters of the central Mediterranean. For the Italians, naval strategy was largely dictated by geography. From its southern naval base at Taranto the Italian battle fleet was well placed to cut this British sea route, and also to protect its own sea lanes between Italy and Libya, its colony in North Africa. Malta lay roughly at the crossroads of these two sea routes – hence the strategic part it would play in the naval campaign. Safeguarding Malta became a key British aim during the war.

For Italy, the second half of 1940 would be dominated by two military campaigns. One would be the lacklustre invasion of British-controlled Egypt by the Italian Army based in Libya. By December, it had advanced barely 50 miles into Egypt, whereupon its commander decided to dig in and hold his forward positions around Sidi Barrani. In late October, the Italians launched an invasion of Greece from Albania, which they had annexed in April 1939. It was equally lacklustre, and the Greeks drove the attackers back across the border. By the end of the year, the Greeks had made significant inroads into Albania. At sea the British and Italian battle fleets had clashed indecisively at the battles of Calabria (or Punta Stilo) in July and Cape Spartivento (or Teulada) in November. Both were encounter battles – the result of British probes into the central Mediterranean from the east and west, respectively.

While neither clash developed into a proper sea battle, the Royal Navy enjoyed a number of minor successes in the waters around Sicily, and on the convoy route between southern Italy and Albania. More importantly, on 11 November an air strike from the aircraft carrier *Illustrious* attacked Taranto, the main base of the Italian battle fleet. Three Italian battleships were sunk or damaged – half of the fleet's capital ships. This emboldened the British, who began venturing into the central Mediterranean in force, running convoys into Malta, naval forces to Gibraltar and even venturing into the Adriatic to bombard the Albanian coast. On land, General Archibald Wavell's Army of the Nile went over onto the offensive in early December, and within a

A depiction of the night action off Matapan, 28 March 1941, showing Cunningham's battleships destroying a force of Italian heavy cruisers. This victory helped ensure that the Regia Marina's battle fleet would not sail in support of the German invasion of Crete, or risk another surface clash with the British in the same waters.

month they had driven the Italians out of Egypt. By early February Benghazi had fallen, and over a quarter of a million Italian troops had been captured. Further south, British and Commonwealth operations in Abyssinia (Ethiopia) were also progressing well. However, all this was about to change.

The first sign of trouble came on 10 January 1941, when the aircraft carrier *Illustrious* was attacked in the Sicilian Narrows. She was hit several times, but managed to limp into Malta, and then on to Alexandria, and so to an American shipyard for repairs. Her assailants were Ju 87 Stukas, 43 aircraft in two air groups, supported by a squadron of ten Italian torpedo bombers. The German squadrons formed part of General Hans Geisler's X.Fliegerkorps, a formation of 350 aircraft, which had been sent to the Mediterranean to bolster the Italians, following the recent setbacks in North Africa. The air crews of X.Fliegerkorps had been especially trained in anti-shipping strikes, and they proved far more effective than their Italian counterparts had been. This gave Cunningham a foretaste of what was to come.

Mussolini's unprovoked invasion of Greece in late 1940 was supposed to mark a necessary first step in the reeastablishment of Italy's ancient Roman empire. By the end of the year, though, the Greeks had counter-attacked, and pushed the Italians back into Albania. This was deeply humiliating for Mussolini, but it worried Hitler too, who was busy laying plans for an invasion of the Soviet Union. To protect his southern flank, and to prop up his fascist ally, Hitler decided to intervene in early 1941. He ordered a German invasion of the Balkans, sweeping through a weak and politically unstable Yugoslavia and on into Greece.

Churchill promised to help Greece, and so, as General Wavell's army was sweeping westwards through Libya, its best troops were ordered to disengage, and to embark on transport ships bound for Greece. This troop movement was codenamed Operation *Lustre*, and was carried out successfully in early March. By then, though, General Erwin Rommel's Afrikakorps was poised

Reinforcements for the Crete garrison being landed in Canea from the Australian light cruiser *Perth* following their evacuation from Greece in late April 1941. Many of these men were poorly equipped, having been evacuated from the Greek mainland, and had little time to ready themselves before the German onslaught on 20 May.

to go onto the offensive in North Africa, where Cyrenaica was now just weakly held. He struck on 24 March, and in less than a month his troops had reached the Egyptian frontier. Meanwhile, German troops were massing on the Yugoslav border. For the moment, though, Cunningham was fully occupied safeguarding the transport of Commonwealth troops to Greece, and protecting the transports from attack by the Regia Marina. It was just as well he was prepared, as in late March, bowing to German pressure, the Regia Marina was ordered to conduct a sweep of the Ionian Sea, in an attempt to disrupt the *Lustre* operation. Instead, it led to a major clash between the British and Italian fleets.

At dawn on 28 March 1941, the Italian fleet was to the west of Crete, and unaware that Cunningham and his own battle fleet was at sea. The first inkling of this came that morning when cruisers of both fleets clashed near the small Cretan island of Gavdos. The British cruisers withdrew when an Italian batleship appeared – Admiral Angelo Iachino's flagship the *Vittorio Veneto*. Throughout the afternoon, the battleship was subjected to repeated strikes launched from the British carrier *Formidable*. Iachino withdrew to the west, but late that afternoon the *Vittorio Veneto* was hit, as was the heavy cruiser *Pola*. The battleship limped away, but Iachino detached a force of cruisers and destroyers to protect the *Pola* and tow her to safety. Using radar, Cunningham's battleships stalked the Italian cruisers in the growing darkness, and just before 2230hrs they opened fire. The one-sided Battle of Matapan was over in minutes, and ended in the loss of three Italian cruisers and two destroyers.

More than the physical loss, Matapan resulted in the Italian fleet ceding control of the eastern Mediterranean to the British. In theory that should have given Cunningham a free hand to do whatever he liked in Greek waters. Instead, any strategic advantage from the victory was lost the moment the Germans launched Operation *Marita*, the codename for their Balkan offensive, which began on 6 April. With the bulk of the Greek Army in Albania, the Metaxas Line fortifications near the Greco-Bulgarian border were relatively lightly defended. The line was quickly overrun, and ten days later, after the Germans had crossed Yugoslavia and into Greece, they outflanked the bulk of the Greek Army in Albania. From mid-April on, the remainder of the Greek and Commonwealth defenders were in full retreat. However, a makeshift defence around Thermopylae held the Germans up long enough for an evacuation to be organized. It then fell to Cunningham to organize this, and to protect the laden troop transports.

By necessity, the evacuation was a hastily organized affair. The military situation was deteriorating too quickly for anything else. Several ports were used, but given the speed of the Axis advance, options were limited. On 24 April, Commonwealth troops were successfully evacuated from Rafti and Rafina near Athens, and from the city's main port of Piraeus. The following day, all remaining RAF squadrons flew to Crete, while their ground staff were evacuated by ship. Then, on 26 April, German parachutists captured Corinth, while to the west other German troops crossed into the Peloponnese. Athens fell on 27 April, but the evacuations continued from Nafplio, Megara, Kalamata and Monemvasia in the Peloponnese. For the most part the troops were spirited away safely, but the destroyers *Diamond* and *Wryneck*, crammed with troops evacuated from Nafplio, were both sunk by Stukas, and over 900 men were lost. The Luftwaffe also sank several troop ships, causing heavy loss of life.

The evacuation ended on 30 April, by which time the Germans had conquered all of the Greek mainland. Small pockets of isolated Allied troops remained, and these eventually surrendered. In the end, over 50,000 Commonwealth troops were evacuated, the majority being shipped to Alexandria. Roughly 21,000 were taken to Crete. About 8,000 more troops were captured in southern Greece, although total Commonwealth losses have been placed at around 15,000 killed or captured. Churchill's intervention in Greece may have been a political and diplomatic necessity, but strategically it was a disaster. It also set the scene for the German invasion of Crete, and for the disaster that befell the Allies there, on both land and sea.

At this point, an attack on Crete was still not a foregone conclusion. Hitler, with his attention focused on Operation *Barbarossa* – his imminent invasion of the Soviet Union – saw the whole Greek campaign as a distraction. Still, with Crete in Allied hands, it could serve as a springboard for an Allied invasion of Greece. More importantly still, Allied bombers based on the island could attack the Romanian oilfields. If Crete were captured, Germany's southern flank would be far more secure. Two days before the fall of Athens, as German troops were still advancing through Greece, Hitler authorized Directive 28 – the invasion of Crete. As the Greek campaign ended, and the Luftwaffe established itself in southern Greek airfields, audacious plans for Operation *Merkur* (*Mercury*) were drawn up. In this operation, the key to success would be air power. In Alexandria, Admiral Cunningham was also laying plans for the naval defence of Crete. He was well aware of the threat posed by the Luftwaffe, and after the attack on *Illustrious* he also knew the potential risk to his ships. However, he was adamant that, come what may, the Royal Navy would play its part in what could well be an extremely dangerous and costly operation.

CHRONOLOGY

1941

Wednesday 14 May   Heavy air attacks on Cretan airfields of Heraklion and Maleme.
Force A (Vice Admiral Sir Henry Pridham-Wippell) sails from Alexandria, to take up position south-west of Crete.

Friday 16 May   Force B sails from Alexandria, with troops embarked to reinforce the Crete garrison.
Forces C and D prepare to sweep the Aegean for enemy invasion convoys.

Saturday 17 May   Heavy air attacks on Heraklion, Maleme and Suda Bay.
Forces C and D recalled to Alexandria to refuel.

Sunday 18 May   Heavy air attacks on Heraklion, Maleme and Suda Bay.
Forces C and D return to their stations to the south and west of Crete.

Monday 19 May   Heavy air attacks on Heraklion, Maleme and Suda Bay.
Force A1 (Rear Admiral Rawlings) relieves Force A to the south-west of Crete.

Tuesday 20 May   Heavy air attacks on Maleme and Suda Bay are followed by parachute and glider landings there.
Parachute landings at Heraklion and Rethymnon.
Forces A1, B, C and D are ordered to prepare for offensive operations.

Wednesday 21 May   Air attacks on Maleme and nearby Canea (Chania) are followed by further German landings.
Rethymnon and Heraklion remain under Allied control.
Heavy fighting continues around Maleme and Canea, but Maleme airfield is captured by nightfall.
Naval units are ordered to enter the Aegean – Rear Admiral Glennie intercepts the Axis invasion force north of Canea.
The destroyer *Juno* is sunk by air attack.

Thursday 22 May   German reinforcements arrive, tipping the balance of the battle in the Axis favour.
A counter-attack towards Maleme is repulsed.
Rear Admiral King's Force C attacks the invasion force south of Milos.
The light cruisers *Naiad* and *Carlisle* are damaged in air attacks.
Rear Admiral Rawlings' Force A1 in the Kythera Strait comes under sustained air attack. Light cruisers *Fiji* and *Gloucester* and destroyer *Greyhound* are sunk, battleships *Warspite* and *Valiant* are damaged.

Friday 23 May   British destroyers attack the invasion force north of Maleme.
0408hrs: Admiral Cunningham orders naval forces to withdraw to Alexandria to refuel.
The destroyers *Kashmir* and *Kelly* are sunk in air attack.
MTBs in Suda Bay are destroyed in air attack.
Heavy Luftwaffe air attacks continue around Maleme and Canea.
Fighting continues around Maleme, Canea and Heraklion.

Saturday 24 May   Fighting continues around Maleme, Canea and Heraklion.
Admiral Cunningham informs his superiors that the Navy cannot continue to operate in the Aegean due to heavy air attacks.

Rear Admiral Bernard Rawlings, commanding the 7th Cruiser Squadron, was one of Admiral Cunningham's most trusted deputies. He would lead the battle fleet into action on 'Black Thursday' (22 May) to help protect the fleet's scattered lighter forces from air attack.

Sunday 25 May	British naval forces conduct a pre-dawn sweep along the north coast of Crete.
	Heavy air attacks around Canea, as fighting continues.
	Significant German reinforcements are brought in to Maleme by air.
	A British air attack strikes Maleme airfield, destroying around 24 German transport planes.
Monday 26 May	British naval forces conduct another pre-dawn sweep along the north coast of Crete.
	An air strike is launched from *Formidable* against the airfield on Scarpanto (Karpathos) in the Aegean.
	Commonwealth troops are driven back around Canea, but hold the enemy at Heraklion.
	Vice Admiral Pridham-Wippell's Force A is attacked – the carrier *Formidable* and destroyer *Nubian* are badly damaged.
Tuesday 27 May	Minelayer *Abdiel* and destroyers *Hero* and *Nizam* land troops at Suda during the night.
	Vice Admiral Pridham-Wippell's force is subjected to heavy air attack, and the battleship *Barham* is damaged.
	Admiral Cunningham recalls Vice Admiral Pridham-Wippell's force to Alexandria.
	The Suda defences collapse, and Allied forces withdraw. The Heraklion sector is still holding.
	The decision is made to withdraw from Crete, and Admiral Cunningham is ordered to support the evacuation.
Wednesday 28 May	Force B (Rear Admiral Rawlings) and Force C (Rear Admiral King) are dispatched from Alexandria to cover the evacuation.
	Allied troops withdraw towards Sphakia, on the southern coast of Crete.
	Further German reinforcements are flown to Heraklion.
	Force B is subjected to heavy air attack – light cruiser *Ajax* is damaged and sent back to Alexandria.
Thursday 29 May	Before dawn, Force C embarks troops from Sphakia, and Force B from Heraklion.
	At dawn, Force B is subjected to heavy air attack – destroyers *Hereward* and *Imperial* are sunk, and light cruisers *Dido* and *Orion* are badly damaged.
	Sphakia is subjected to heavy air attack.
	Remnants of forces B and C arrive in Alexandria and disembark evacuated troops.
	Force D (Rear Admiral Glennie) sails from Alexandria, bound for Sphakia.
	Admiral Cunningham decides that, regardless of the mounting losses, the evacuation will continue.
Friday 30 May	During night, Force D embarks troops from Sphakia.
	German troops begin to attack the Allied defensive perimeter around Sphakia.
	Force D comes under sustained air attacks as it withdraws, and the light cruiser *Perth* is damaged.
	Force C (Rear Admiral King) leaves Alexandria, bound for Sphakia.
	Force D arrives in Alexandria and disembarks evacuated troops.
Saturday 31 May	During night, Force C embarks troops from Sphakia.
	Force C comes under sustained air attack as it withdraws, but Allied fighter protection helps protect the warships. However, the destroyer *Napier* is damaged.
	Force D (Rear Admiral Glennie) departs from Alexandria, to conduct a final evacuation.
	Force C arrives in Alexandria and disembarks evacuated troops.
	Admiral Cunningham is told by General Wavell that any troops left in Crete after the final evacuation will be ordered to surrender.
Sunday 1 June	During night, Force D embarks a final body of troops from Sphakia.
	Force D withdraws safely, but light anti-aircraft (AA) cruiser *Calcutta*, sent to support it, is attacked by enemy aircraft, and is sunk before it can rendezvous with Rear Admiral Glennie's force.
	Force D arrives in Alexandria and disembarks the final batch of evacuated troops.

OPPOSING COMMANDERS

ALLIED

The fate of the Mediterranean Fleet during the naval battle for Crete rested on one very competent pair of shoulders. **Admiral Andrew B. Cunningham** (1883–1963), or 'ABC' as he was known in the service, took command of the Mediterranean Fleet in June 1939, and flew his flag in the battleship *Warspite*. Cunningham was already an experienced Mediterranean hand, having commanded a destroyer there in World War I, and the Mediterranean Fleet's destroyers during the interwar years. Shortly before World War II, he served as the fleet's second-in-command, under Admiral Dudley Pound. Cunningham possessed great courage and resolution, but he was also a highly intelligent commander, with an immense sense of foresight. He relished a challenge, and showed a steely resolution when under pressure. His subordinates and superiors alike often found him difficult – he had a bullying side to him, and he disliked 'yes men'. This, though, simply encouraged his staff and subordinates to excel, as their commander expected nothing less.

Admiral Andrew B. Cunningham (or 'ABC' to his men) was a hard taskmaster, and during the Crete campaign he pushed his ships and men to their limits. Without his determination, though, it would have been unlikely that so many of the Crete garrison could have been rescued.

During the evacuation from Greece and Crete, he showed determination to the point of recklessness, but for the most part his gamble paid off. He was also charming and diplomatic – skills he used to the full in mid-1940, when he persuaded the commander of the French squadron in Alexandria to peacefully intern his ships. He could also be kind and welcoming – the house he and his wife shared in Alexandria was often full of naval guests, from junior officers to admirals. Cunningham was made Admiral of the Fleet in 1943, and went on to oversee the Allied landings in Sicily and Italy, and the surrender of the Italian battle fleet. He subsequently served as First Sea Lord until he retired from the service in 1946. Cunningham was very much the right man for the job. It

The second-in-command of the Mediterranean Fleet, 56-year-old Vice Admiral Sir Henry Pridham-Wippell, was the senior officer at sea during the opening days of the Crete campaign. Like his superior, Pridham-Wippell was a highly experienced and gifted commander, but had no means to counter the threat posed by the Luftwaffe.

would be hard to think of anyone better qualified to command the Mediterranean Fleet in time of crisis.

Assisting him during the campaign were a number of exceptionally skilled subordinates. The most significant of these was **Vice Admiral Henry Pridham-Wippell** (1885–1952). As the second-in-command of the Mediterranean Fleet he was Cunningham's deputy, and commanded the fleet's light forces. On 12 May, on the eve of the Crete campaign, he was given command of the fleet's battle squadron, and shifted his flag into the battleship *Queen Elizabeth*. Pridham-Wippell had been friends with 'ABC' since they served on destroyers in the Dardanelles together, and both respected each other's professionalism. Pridham-Wippell had performed exceptionally well during the previous winter, when he took his cruisers on a sweep into the Adriatic, and displayed initiative and courage during the recent Battle of Matapan. In short, he was a thoroughly reliable deputy to 'ABC', and a commander who enjoyed his superior's complete confidence.

Rear Admiral Bernard Rawlings and **Rear Admiral Edward King**, commanded the fleet's cruiser squadrons during the campaign, while **Rear Admiral Irvine Glennie** commanded Cunningham's destroyers. All three were highly experienced naval officers, and could be relied upon in a crisis. Equally skilled was the Canadian-born **Rear Admiral Tom Baillie-Grohman**, another old friend of Cunningham's, who was attached to the staff of the General Officer Commanding (GOC) Middle East. Essentially, this meant he was there to coordinate the evacuation from Greece, and was responsible for setting in train a similar rescue of the army during the Crete campaign. Cunningham was fortunate to have such capable subordinates during the spring of 1941.

The GOC Middle East at the time was **General Archibald Wavell**. He first saw action during the Boer War, and during World War I he fought in France, where he received the Military Cross. He was sent to the Middle East a month after Cunningham, and so the two commanders had time to build up a decent working relationship. It was Wavell who masterminded Operation *Compass* – the dramatic assault on the Italian Army in the Western Desert. However, he failed to stand up to Churchill when he was ordered to send his best troops to Greece, and so his army in Libya was too weak to stop Rommel's own offensive. With his troops bundled out of Libya, then Greece and finally Crete, Wavell fell from grace in London. When Operation *Battleaxe* – his attempt to relieve Tobruk – failed that June, Wavell was replaced by General Claude Auchinleck. During the Crete campaign, Wavell oversaw the campaign from his headquarters in Cairo.

In Crete, Wavell's man on the spot was **Major-General Bernard Freyberg**. He distinguished himself during World War I, winning the Victoria Cross on the Western Front. In 1939, he became the commander of the New Zealand

Expeditionary Force, and commanded the New Zealand Division during the Greek campaign. Freyberg and the survivors of his command were evacuated to Crete, where the general was given command of the island's defences. His unwillingness to realize that the enemy might attack from the air contributed to the Commonwealth defeat on Crete. Still, Freyberg supervised the withdrawal and evacuation of the survivors of 'Creforce', and afterwards he was promoted and continued to command the New Zealanders deployed in North Africa.

The Air Officer Commanding-in-Chief during the campaign was **Air Chief Marshal Sir Arthur Longmore**, based in Egypt. Longmore had been a naval officer and aviator during World War I, but transferred to the RAF in 1920. He held a range of commands during the interwar years, before being given his Middle Eastern command in April 1940. During the Greek and Crete campaigns he struggled with the lack of resources available to him, but was prepared to act aggressively when required. His constant demands for reinforcements during the two campaigns led to a rift with Churchill, who replaced Longmore with Air Marshal Arthur Tedder on 1 June 1941. Longmore retired from the service the following year. While Cunningham criticized the RAF for the lack of air support given to his fleet during the Crete campaign, Longmore only had a handful of squadrons available to him, and their aircraft were greatly outnumbered and often outclassed by their Luftwaffe opponents.

AXIS

Admiral Cunningham's nemesis in the Crete campaign was **General der Flieger Baron Wolfram von Richthofen** (1895–1945), the commander of the Luftwaffe's VIII.Fliegerkorps. The young Prussian nobleman served with the cavalry for much of World War I, but in 1917 his cousin Manfred ('The Red Baron') persuaded Wolfram to join the Luftstreitkräfte (Imperial Air

General der Flieger Freiherr ('Baron') Wolfram von Richthofen (right) commanded the Luftwaffe's VIII.Fliegerkorps during the Crete campaign. During World War I he served with his famous cousin, 'The Red Baron', and subsequently gave service in both the Spanish Civil War and the France 1940 campaign.

Service). On his first mission over the Western Front in 1918, he witnessed the death of Manfred, but Wolfram survived, and ended the war as an ace with eight 'kills'. After the war he became a civilian, but returned to military service in the early 1930s, when he joined the Luftwaffe. There he became an advocate of dive-bombing, and was responsible for building up and training the Luftwaffe's dive-bomber fleet

He subsequently saw action is Spain, and by the outbreak of war in 1939 Richthofen commanded VIII.Fliegerkorps, which specialized in ground-attack operations. He commanded the Fliegerkorps in Poland in 1939 and France in 1940, both during the invasion of France and during the Battle of Britain. By then, he had developed a reputation as being a highly competent air commander, with a ruthless ability to direct his squadrons where they would inflict the maximum damage on the enemy. He also noted the heavy losses his aircraft suffered during the Battle of Britain, and evolved new tactics to better protect his dive-bombers.

During the Balkan and Greek campaigns, Richthofen concentrated on the destruction of enemy command centres, and attacks on enemy troop columns. Then, from mid-April, his primary target became the merchant and naval ships involved in the Allied evacuation from Greece. After Greece was overrun, Richthofen established his squadrons in airfields across southern Greece and the Aegean, and so was well placed to attack Cunningham's warships when they ventured within range.

Before the war, General der Flieger Kurt Student developed the Luftwaffe's Fallschirmjäger (paratrooper) force, and commanded it during the attacks on Holland and Belgium in 1940, and in the air assault on Crete the following year. After the war, he was convicted of war crimes following his treatment of both Allied prisoners and civilians on Crete.

Generalmajor Kurt Student (1890–1978) commanded the air assault on Crete, and the Luftwaffe forces charged with establishing air superiority over the island. In 1913, Student became a pilot in the German Army, and scored his first kill over the Western Front in the summer of 1916. He ended the war as a squadron leader, with six confirmed kills. During the interwar years, he supervised the development of military gliders, before transferring to the newly formed Luftwaffe, where he was responsible for the training of pilots. In the summer of 1938, he became the commander of a fledgling airborne troop organization, which evolved into Germany's first Fallschirmjäger or parachute division. In the spring of 1940, Student and his Fallschirmjäger saw action in Denmark, Norway, the Netherlands and Belgium. The highlight of this campaign was the capture of the Belgian stronghold of Eben Emael, an operation planned by Student himself.

Student was decorated, promoted and given a new command – XI.Fliegerkorps. This combined an expanded airborne assault force with its squadrons of transport planes, and attached them to a more conventional Luftwaffe air group, with its own fighters and bombers. For the Crete operation, officially Richthofen commanded his own Fliegerkorps, as well as Student's XI.Fliegerkorps, and elements of IV.Fliegerkorps, under the command of General der Flieger Alexander Löhr. Of these, it would be Richthofen's own VIII.Fliegerkorps that would primarily operate against the Mediterranean Fleet.

OPPOSING FORCES

The naval battle for Crete was part of a larger struggle, fought on land as well as at sea and in the air. While our main emphasis will focus on the naval side of this brief and bloody campaign, we also need to set the naval struggle in context. The fighting on Crete itself has already been the focus of a book in this series (Campaign 147: *Crete 1941*), so little more needs to be said on this aspect of the story. However, where relevant, passing mention will need to be made of the land battle, in order to provide the full picture, and to fully explain why the naval contest was so important. This also applies to this description of the forces involved. A more detailed outline of the land forces, and the air assets assigned to them, can be found in the Campaign title mentioned above. This allows us to concentrate on the heart of this book – the struggle between the Luftwaffe and the Royal Navy.

ALLIED

In mid-May 1941, the Mediterranean Fleet had begun to suffer the brunt of Luftwaffe attention, both in the waters of Sicily and Malta, and in the Aegean. The recent arrival of reinforcements had strengthened the fleet, which now boasted five capital ships: four Queen Elizabeth-class battleships (*Barham*, *Queen Elizabeth*, *Valiant* and *Warspite*), and the Illustrious-class fleet aircraft carrier *Formidable*. This carrier had neatly replaced her badly damaged sister ship *Illustrious*, which had been patched up in Malta and Alexandria, before being sent off through the Suez Canal for full repairs in Norfolk, VA. It would be mid-December before she returned to active service.

In fact, even *Formidable* was effectively out of operation due to a chronic lack of aircraft. She had joined the Mediterranean Fleet in early March, but since then she had seen action at Matapan, been involved in the fleet's bombardment of Tripoli, and supported the critical passage of the much-needed 'Tiger convoy' through the Mediterranean. This all led to attrition through loss, damage or mechanical problems to her embarked aircraft. As a result, when the Crete campaign began, she only had four operational Fulmar fighter aircraft available. It would be the end of the month before reinforcements reached her, or her existing aircraft would be fully repaired. She would then play her part in the naval battle for Crete, and pay a hefty price for it. So, of the fleet's capital ships, only the four battleships were fully operational, and ready to play their part in the naval defence of Crete.

At the time, the Mediterranean Fleet's battle squadron consisted of four Queen Elizabeth-class battleships. Here, *Valiant, Queen Elizabeth* and *Barham* are pictured from the deck of the fourth ship in the line, *Warspite*. Their primary role during the Crete campaign was to counter the threat posed by the Italian battle fleet.

Admiral Cunningham had several light cruisers available to him, but no heavy cruisers, as due to their impressive range the Admiralty felt they were better suited to service elsewhere, protecting ocean convoys, and patrolling the northern approaches to the Atlantic. At the time, there were five light cruisers in the Mediterranean Fleet: two Leander-class (*Ajax* and *Orion*), and three light cruisers that were namesakes of their class – *Gloucester*, the newly arrived *Fiji* (which had joined the fleet with the Tiger convoy) and the Royal Australian Navy (RAN) *Perth*. As the 15th Cruiser Squadron, all but *Fiji* were veterans of Matapan. Even more useful in the coming fight were the fleet's six anti-aircraft cruisers. Three of these (*Carlisle, Calcutta* and *Coventry*) were old Carlisle-class vessels, converted World War I-era light cruisers. The other three (*Dido, Naiad* and *Phoebe*) were modern Dido-class vessels, purpose-built AA cruisers, designed to protect the fleet from air attack. They would prove their worth in the waters off Crete.

The Mediterranean Fleet also boasted a large quantity of destroyers. Despite the fleet's destroyers suffering losses during the evacuation of the army from Greece, Admiral Cunningham still had 30 of them at his disposal. Most of them were fairly modern ones: 14 J/K/N-class destroyers (*Juno, Janus, Jervis, Jackal, Jaguar, Kelly, Kandahar, Kingston, Kipling, Kashmir, Kelvin, Kimberley, Napier* and *Nizam*), built between 1938 and 1940, and ten G/H/I-class vessels (*Griffin, Greyhound, Hero, Hostspur, Hereward, Hasty, Havock, Isis, Imperial* and *Ilex)* built during the mid-1930s. The handful of others, apart from the Tribal-class destroyer *Nubian*, were slightly older ships. Two C/D-class ships (*Decoy* and *Defender*) were built in the early 1930s, while the Scott-class flotilla leader *Stuart*, and the V/W-class destroyers *Vendetta* and *Voyager*, were all built during or just after World War I. These last three were operated by the Royal Australian Navy.

Most of these warships, from battleships down to destroyers, suffered from having a relatively poor AA capability. The High-Angle Control System (HACS) was designed to coordinate the barrage fire from a ship's large AA guns. The aim was to throw up a devastating wall of AA fire, forcing the attacker to turn away or risk the near certainty of being hit. This might work against high-flying level bombers, but it was little use when facing enemy dive-bombers, as the dive threw off the system's fire control calculations. In fact, the whole system proved less effective than its designers had hoped.

Still, the fire from these guns could act as a deterrent, and during the campaign it was demonstrably effective in keeping enemy bombers at bay, at least until the ammunition ran out. That in itself was a problem. Many warships had expended all or most of their ammunition during the Greek evacuation. There was only enough stock in Alexandria to replenish three-quarters of this expended ammunition. So, many of the ships were short of AA shells when the campaign for Crete began.

More effective were the 5.25in. dual-purpose guns of the Dido class, especially when operated in conjunction with the ships' fire control radar as well as HACS. Although designed to carry five twin turrets, only *Naiad* was fully armed – due to shortages *Dido* and *Phoebe* lacked 'Q' turret, so only had eight guns apiece rather than ten. Still, these ships demonstrated their effectiveness during the campaign. Also useful were the older Carlisle-class AA cruisers, armed with 4in. quick-firing guns. Their guns, though, had a slower rate of fire than the larger 5.25in. guns, and a more restrictive elevation.

The smaller-range weapons in the fleet were primarily 2-pdr (40mm) pom-poms carried in multi-barrelled mounts or 0.5in. machine guns, also in four-barrelled mountings. While both put up an impressive volume of fire, these weapons were of relatively limited use due to their short range. Still, they did manage to shoot down attacking aircraft during the campaign, particularly when dive-bombers were committed to their attack dive, immediately over the target ship. During the campaign, what became clear was that apart from the Dido-class ships, which had the firepower needed to properly defend themselves as well as nearby ships, the warships Admiral Cunningham sent into action off Crete lacked adequate protection against air attacks. Of course, when most of these ships were built, few could have predicted that the vessels would be subjected to the level of air attacks they encountered during the Crete campaign.

Without *Formidable* fully operational, the Mediterranean Fleet lacked dedicated air support. Only a handful of drastically under-strength RAF squadrons were available. Two of these (30 Sqn and 203 Sqn) were bomber units, equipped with Bristol Blenheim medium bombers. The remaining three units based in Crete (33 Sqn, 80 Sqn and 112 Sqn) were fighter squadrons, equipped with obsolete Gloster Gladiators, augmented by a few Hawker Hurricanes. Many of these, though, had suffered maintenance

While most Commonwealth cruisers and destroyers mounted larger calibre guns for anti-aircraft protection, they also carried point defence weapons. One of these was the 0.5in. machine gun, which was used in multiple four-barrelled or eight-barrelled mounts. These weapons, though, lacked the range and stopping power needed to offer a real deterrent to enemy bombers.

The C/D-class destroyer HMS *Defender* entered service in the early 1930s, and saw extensive action during the first months of the naval campaign in the Mediterranean. *Defender* was involved in both the evacuation from Greece and then Crete, but was eventually bombed and sunk the following July, while running supplies into Tobruk.

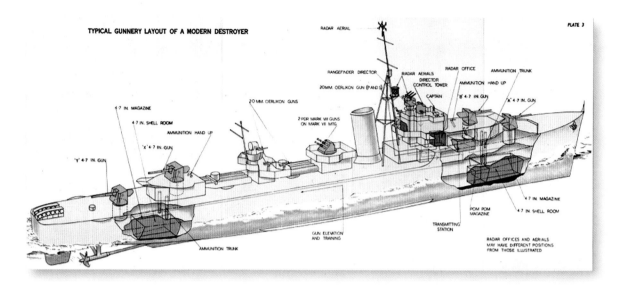

TYPICAL GUNNERY LAYOUT OF A MODERN DESTROYER

PLATE 3

RADAR AERIAL

RANGEFINDER DIRECTOR
20MM OERLIKON GUN (P AND S)
20 MM OERLIKON GUNS
DIRECTOR CONTROL TOWER
RADAR AERIALS
RADAR OFFICE
CAPTAIN
AMMUNITION TRUNK
AMMUNITION HAND UP
'B' 4.7 IN. GUN
'A' 4.7 IN. GUN

4.7 IN. MAGAZINE
4.7 IN. SHELL ROOM
AMMUNITION HAND UP
'X' 4.7 IN. GUN
2 PDR MARK VIII GUNS ON MARK VII MTG

'Y' 4.7 IN. GUN

4.7 IN. MAGAZINE
4.7 IN. SHELL ROOM
POM POM MAGAZINE
TRANSMITTING STATION

GUN ELEVATION AND TRAINING

AMMUNITION TRUNK

RADAR OFFICES AND AERIALS MAY HAVE DIFFERENT POSITIONS FROM THOSE ILLUSTRATED

Most of the Commonwealth destroyers which took part in the naval battle for Crete were of the J/K/N class, which entered service from 1939 onwards. Their anti-aircraft armament consisted of both their main 4.7in. guns, guided by the HACS director, as well as closer-range weapons, such as the multiple 2-pdr pom-pom and machine-gun mountings. The 20mm Oerlikon mounts post-dated the Crete campaign, and were used to replace the less effective machine guns.

problems following the Greek campaign, and were not fully operational. It was estimated that no more than 18 of these aircraft were available at the time. Also at Crete's Maleme airfield was Commander Beale's small detachment of Fleet Air Arm planes and their maintenance crews from 805 Sqn – three Sea Gladiators and three Fairey Fulmars. They, at least, had fuel, ammunition and equipment, which gave them the edge over many of their RAF counterparts.

In terms of land forces, Major-General Freyberg's 'Creforce' consisted of a mixed bag of British, New Zealand, Australian and Greek troops from various formations. These included the island's original British and Greek garrison, bolstered by the 25,000 men who had recently been evacuated

The crew of a destroyer on AA watch. Their dress indicates this photograph was taken in Arctic waters, but the procedure was the same, regardless of the theatre. The crew would hold two watches, and if Action Stations were called, the whole crew would be required to defend the ship. The weapon mounted amidships is a quadruple 2-pdr pom-pom.

to Greece from the Greek mainland. Up to 10,000 of these evacuees were non-combatants, and so of little use to Freyberg, but they also included two brigades of his own 2nd New Zealand Division, an Australian brigade and a British brigade. The bulk of the non-combatants were evacuated to Egypt before the campaign began, but a number still remained. In all, Freyberg commanded roughly 30,000 Commonwealth troops (15,000 British, 7,500 New Zealanders and 6,500 Australians), as well as 10,000 Greeks. Many of these men, though, lacked the heavy support weapons and ammunition reserves that might have made a real difference in the battle when it came.

ALLIED ORDER OF BATTLE

Note: The composition of the Allied naval forces varied during the campaign. The strengths of the forces listed below are given when they were formed. Changes which occurred during the campaign are described later, in the account of the fighting.

MEDITERRANEAN FLEET (ADMIRAL ANDREW B. CUNNINGHAM)

FORCE A (VICE ADMIRAL HENRY PRIDHAM-WIPPELL)

Queen Elizabeth (Captain Barry) – Queen Elizabeth-class battleship, flagship
Barham (Captain Cooke) – Queen Elizabeth-class battleship
Jervis (Captain Mack) – J/K/N-class destroyer
Jaguar (Lieutenant-Commander Hine) – J/K/N-class destroyer (attached to Force A1)
Nizam (Lieutenant-Commander Clark) – J/K/N-class destroyer (attached to Force E)
Defender (Lieutenant-Commander Farnfield) – C/D-class destroyer
Imperial (Lieutenant-Commander de Winton Kitcat) – G/H/I-class destroyer (attached to Force B)

FORCE A1 (REAR ADMIRAL BERNARD RAWLINGS)

Warspite (Captain Fisher) – Queen Elizabeth-class battleship, flagship
Valiant (Captain Morgan) – Queen Elizabeth-class battleship
Greyhound (Commander Marshall-A'Deane) – G/H/I-class destroyer
Griffin (Lieutenant Lee-Barber) – G/H/I-class destroyer
Havock (Lieutenant Watkins) – G/H/I-class destroyer
Hero (Commander Briggs) – G/H/I-class destroyer
Jaguar (Lieutenant-Commander Hine) – J/K/N-class destroyer (detached from Force A)

FORCE B (CAPTAIN HENRY ROWLEY – KIA)

Gloucester (Captain Rowley) – Gloucester-class light cruiser, flagship
Fiji (Captain William-Powlett) – Fiji-class light cruiser
Orion (Captain Back) – Leander-class light cruiser
Dido (Captain McCall) – Dido-class light AA cruiser (attached to Force D)
Decoy (Commander McGregor) – D-class destroyer
Hereward (Lieutenant Munn) – G/H/I-class destroyer
Hotspur (Lieutenant-Commander Brown) – G/H/I-class destroyer
Imperial (Lieutenant-Commander de Winton Kitcat) – G/H/I-class destroyer (detached from Force A)
Jackal (Lieutenant-Commander Jonas) – J/K/N-class destroyer
Kimberley (Lieutenant-Commander Richardson) – J/K/N-class destroyer

FORCE C (REAR ADMIRAL EDWARD KING)

Naiad (Captain Kelsey) – Dido-class light AA cruiser, flagship
Perth (Captain Bowyer-Smith) – Sydney-class light cruiser
Calcutta (Captain Lees) – Carlisle-class light AA cruiser
Kandahar (Commander Robson) – J/K/N-class destroyer
Nubian (Commander Ravenhill) – Tribal-class destroyer
Kingston (Lieutenant-Commander Somerville) – J/K/N-class destroyer
Juno (Commander Tyrwhitt) – J/K/N-class destroyer

The Operations Room of a wartime destroyer was below decks, where information from radar, radio and the navigator were gathered. The job of the Plotting Officer was to understand the flow of information, and to update the captain on tactical developments. This left the destroyer's captain free to 'fight' his ship from the bridge.

FORCE D (REAR ADMIRAL IRVINE GLENNIE)

Dido (Captain McCall) – Dido-class light AA cruiser, flagship (detached from Force B)
Orion (Captain William-Powlett) – Leander-class light cruiser (detached from Force B)
Ajax (Captain McCarthy) – Leander-class light cruiser
Janus (Commander Tothill) – J/K/N-class destroyer
Hasty (Lieutenant-Commander Tyrwhitt) – G/H/I-class destroyer
Hereward (Lieutenant-Commander Munn) – G/H/I-class destroyer (detached from Force B)
Kimberley (Lieutenant-Commander Richardson) – J/K/N-class destroyer (detached from Force B)

FORCE E (CAPTAIN PHILIP MACK)

Carlisle (Captain Hampton) – Carlisle-class light AA cruiser
Jervis (Captain Mack, CO 14th Destroyer Flotilla) – J/K/N-class destroyer, flagship (detached from Force A)
Ilex (Captain Nicholson) –G/H/I-class destroyer
Nizam (Lieutenant-Commander Clark) – J/K/N-class destroyer (detached from Force A)
Kelly (Captain Mountbatten, CO 15th Destroyer Flotilla) – J/K/N-class destroyer
Kashmir (Commander King) – J/K/N-class destroyer
Kelvin (Commander Alison) – J/K/N-class destroyer
Jackal (Lieutenant-Commander Jonas) – J/K/N-class destroyer (detached from Force B)
Kipling (Commander St Clair-Ford) – J/K/N-class destroyer

AXIS

The air assault on Crete would be carried out by XI.Fliegerkorps, commanded by Generalmajor Kurt Student. It consisted of three air groups, equipped with 530 Ju 52 transport planes. These would be used to transport the airborne troops to Crete. The Fliegerkorps had been formed specifically to provide air transport for German parachutists, and so it was officially based at Berlin Tempelhof airport, where Germany's airborne troops were raised and trained. The Fliegerkorps also incorporated a Wehrmacht glider formation, 22.Luftlande-Division (22nd Air Landing Division), which had begun the war as an infantry formation, before its men were retrained as an air assault division during the winter of 1939/40. It was equipped with 72 DFS 230 gliders. However, during the Crete campaign the division itself would be held in reserve, and the gliders used by other formations.

During the battle for Crete, the Fliegerkorps would transport the parachutists of 7.Flieger-Division, which had been formed by Student in the autumn of 1938. It saw a limited action in April 1940 during the invasion of Denmark and Norway, but its real test came the following month, during the invasion of Belgium and Holland. The division met with mixed success – the spectacular capture of Fort Eben Emael was balanced by a poor performance around The Hague. During Operation *Maritsa* – the invasion of Greece – the parachutists would successfully capture the crossings over the Corinth Canal, and so cut the Allied defences in two. Supporting the assault would be the 5.Gebirgs-Division (5th Mountain Division), which would be brought in by sea, and by air transport after the parachutists had secured the Cretan airfields. In all, the 10,000 parachutists and 750 glider troops who formed the first waves of the airborne assault would be reinforced by another 12,000 men from the mountain division. Thanks to the Royal Navy, many of these reinforcements would never reach Crete.

While on the ground there was something akin to a parity between the two sides, in the air the Germans enjoyed an overwhelming superiority in numbers. Leaving aside the 530 transport planes of XI.Fliegerkorps, the real teeth of the campaign lay in the aircraft of VIII.Fliegerkorps, a veteran air corps commanded by Baron Wolfram von Richthofen, the cousin of 'The Red Baron', Germany's greatest air ace of World War I. He had 716 combat aircraft at his disposal, a formidable mixture of 180 fighters, 268 dive-bombers and 239 conventional bombers, as well as 29 reconnaissance aircraft. It was this air armada that would take on Cunningham's Mediterranean Fleet, as well as providing air support for Student's airborne invasion force.

Following the conquest of Greece, the Luftwaffe quickly secured the Greek airfields, and either expanded them or built new forward ones, within easy reach of Crete. The islands of Leros, Milos and Scarpanto (Karpathos) in the Aegean provided suitable air bases. So, too, did the island of Rhodes, where the Italian Regia Aeronautica had already based small *gruppi* of fighters and torpedo-bombers. Instead, though, Richthofen concentrated his aircraft at Malaoi, Mycenae and Argos in the eastern Peloponnese, and Eleusis and Tatoi, on the western and northern outskirts of Athens. KG 2 was based at Tatoi, LG 1 at Eleusis, StG 2 and JG 77 at Malaoi, StG 77 and ZG 26 at Argos and StG 1 and StG 3 at Mycenae. That placed the bulk of Richthofen's Stukas within 150 miles of Suda Bay in north-western Crete – just over an hour's flying time. From Malaoi, a Stuka carrying a 500kg bomb could range some 320nm out into the Mediterranean, well to the south and east of Crete. That made the entire naval theatre the hunting ground of Richthofen's pilots.

Finally, the Kriegsmarine's commander in the region was Admiral Karlgeorg Schuster. Although he had no German warships at his disposal, he did have a few Italian ones, grudgingly supplied by the Regia Marina, and a small contingent of Kriegsmarine officers and men. These small Italian warships, together with hastily commandeered Greek fishing boats ('caiques'), would form the only naval part of the operation. Essentially, Student was unable to transport the heavy support weapons he needed in Crete by air. So, he called on Schuster to organize their transport by sea. These convoys would also transport a number of Student's reinforcements from 5.Gebirgs-Division. The admiral duly chose the island of Milos as the assembly point of his convoys, and set about gathering the caiques he needed.

In theory, the Axis could also expect the support of the Italian battle fleet. However, after its defeat off Matapan the previous month, the Supermarina – the high command of the Regia Marina – were

A Luftwaffe Ju 88 twin-engined light bomber, laden with four externally mounted SC250 bombs. These 250kg high-explosive bombs were used by both VIII.Fliegerkorps' light bombers and its Stuka dive-bombers, and could be fused to detonate on impact, or following a delay of up to 17 seconds.

Kampfgeschwader 2 'Holzhammer' was equipped with 108 of these Dornier Do 17 twin-engined light bombers. They could carry four 250kg bombs, and they could range up to 360 miles from their airfield at Tatoi outside Athens. This ability also made them particularly useful as reconnaissance aircraft during the Crete campaign.

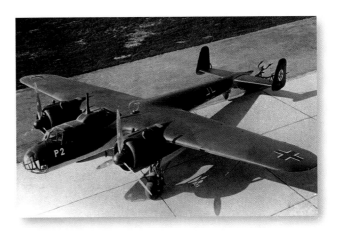

A Junkers Ju 88 bomber, of the type used by two air *Gruppen* of Oberst Knust's LG 1. These were used extensively to attack the Mediterranean Fleet during the naval campaign, as their long range of up to 970 miles allowed them to harry British warships virtually anywhere in the Eastern Mediterranean.

reluctant to commit their battle fleet outside the central Mediterranean. Instead, the Italian naval commitment to the operation was limited to a pair of Spica-class torpedo boats (*Lupo* and *Sagittario*), a half flotilla of MAS motor torpedo boats and a few minesweepers and patrol boats, stationed in the Aegean. The presence of the Italian battle fleet, operating under the air umbrella of the Luftwaffe, might well have made a real difference to the campaign. The Supermarina, though, correctly assumed the British would prefer to operate under cover of darkness. They were well aware that their own crews had less experience of fighting at night than their British counterparts. So, the decision was made not to place the battle fleet at risk in the naval battle for Crete. Admiral Schuster then, would have to make do with the limited resources he already had.

AXIS ORDER OF BATTLE

LUFTWAFFE VIII.FLIEGERKORPS (GENERAL DER FLIEGER BARON WOLFRAM VON RICHTHOFEN)

Note: Typically, each *Gruppe* (air group) consisted of three *Staffel* (squadron) formations, each of approximately 12 bombers or 15 fighters, divided into flights of three aircraft.

Jadgeschwader 77 'Herz' (Major Bernhard Woldenga)
Two air groups (II./JG 77, III./JG 77) of fighters (a total of 90 Me 109 F2s)
Zerstörergeschwader 26 'Horst Wessel' (Oberst Johann Schalk)
Two air groups (II./ZG 26, III./ZG 26) of heavy fighters (a total of 90 Me 110 C4s)
Kampfgeschwader 2 'Holzhammer' (Oberst Herbert Reikoff)
Three air groups (I./KG 2, II./KG 2, III./KG 2) of light bombers (108 Do 17 Z2s)
Lehrgeschwader 1 (Oberst Knust)
Two air groups (I./LG 1, III./LG 1) of light bombers (75 Ju 88 A5s)
One air group (II./LG 1) of medium bombers (36 He 111 H3s)
Sturzkampfgeschwader 1 (Oberst Walter Hagen)
Two air groups (I./StG 1, II./StG 1) of dive-bombers (72 Ju 87 R2 Stukas)
Sturzkampfgeschwader 2 'Immelman' (Oberst Oskar Dinort)
Three air groups (I./StG 2, II./StG 2, III./StG 2) of dive-bombers (108 Ju 87 R2 Stukas)
Sturzkampfgeschwader 3 (Oberst Karl Christ)
One air group (I./StG 3) of dive-bombers (36 Ju 87 R2 Stukas)
Sturzkampfgeschwader 77 (Major Clemens von Schönborn-Wiesentheid)
Two air groups (I./StG 77, II./StG 77) of dive-bombers (72 Ju 87 R2 Stukas)

OPPOSING PLANS

ALLIED

For Admiral Cunningham, his whole strategy centred around sea power. For him, that meant re-establishing control of the sea route through the Mediterranean, from Gibraltar to the Suez Canal. He realized that the Italians temporarily dominated the central Mediterranean, which is why he considered Malta such an important island bastion. It helped protect his own sea route, while lying astride the enemy ones between Italy and Libya. After the Battle of Matapan, he felt he had now established control over the eastern Mediterranean. Similarly, the waters of the western Mediterranean were now largely dominated by Royal Naval forces based in Gibraltar. His problem lay in the centre, where the Italians still had the naval power to deny control of the sea to the British. More significantly, they, together with their German allies, had also demonstrated their ability to vigorously contest any British attempt to force convoys through the Sicilian Narrows leading to Malta, and then on to Alexandria.

For Admiral Cunningham, the Greek campaign was an unwanted distraction to his real objective outlined above. This said, he was well aware where his other duties lay. He felt that the Royal Navy had a traditional responsibility to transport the British Army wherever it needed to go, and to keep it supplied. He also saw it as his fleet's job to evacuate the army again if the need arose, as it had from Norway and Dunkirk the previous year. As he said in a signal sent on the evening of 22 May, while his ships were suffering a grievous mauling off Crete: 'Stick it out. Navy must not let army down.' This was to be his guiding principle throughout the evacuation from Greece, and then the Crete debacle – his fleet must support the army, come what may.

This emphasis on inter-service support was reiterated in his famous statement of 26 May, from which his sentence about rebuilding a fleet and naval tradition has often been misquoted. He prefaced it with this statement: 'It has always been

German paratroops jumping from their Ju 52 transport planes during the airborne invasion of Crete. Although the Mediterranean Fleet could do little to prevent an airborne attack against the island, Cunningham was determined to prevent any seaborne invasion, regardless of the cost to his fleet.

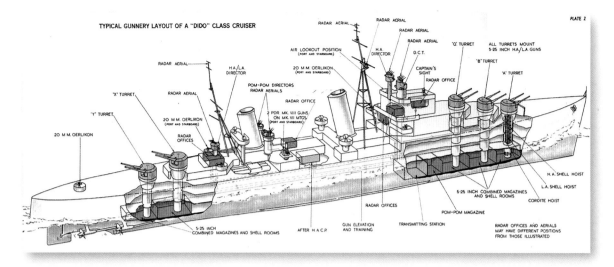

TYPICAL GUNNERY LAYOUT OF A "DIDO" CLASS CRUISER

PLATE 2

The layout of one of the Royal Navy's Dido-class AA cruisers. Although supply problems during fitting out meant that the armament varied slightly, most of the class carried these effective 5.25in. high-angle (HA) dual-purpose guns, their fire directed by the HACS director mounted behind the cruiser's bridge. *Dido, Naiad* and *Phoebe* would all play a part in the campaign.

the duty of the Navy to take the army overseas to battle, and if the army fails, to bring them back again.' Despite all his efforts, Cunningham and his fleet had been unable to prevent the airborne invasion of Crete. Now, as the land campaign reached its climax, he was willing to reiterate to his army counterpart General Wavell that his fleet would also be fully prepared to extricate the Crete garrison, if the need arose. At that stage, though, the fleet was still trying to prevent any further amphibious assaults on the island – part of a defensive plan Cunningham had put into place two weeks before. It showed great flexibility to consider redeploying his naval forces at short notice, to fulfil this new task of extricating the army.

When Cunningham returned to Alexandria on 12 May, having supervised Operation *Tiger*, he was given Ultra intelligence reports which suggested that the German air assault on Crete could begin within three days. Two days later, on 14 May, the island came under heavy air attack from VIII.Fliegerkorps. Cunningham's staff had already drafted a plan for the naval defence of the island. On 14 May, Cunningham put it into effect. Essentially, it involved the stationing of several naval forces around Crete, where they would be poised to intercept any amphibious invasion force, should it appear. He fully realized this was a huge gamble, as the Germans enjoyed overwhelming superiority in the air. Still, it was a risk he had to take, if the Crete garrison were to survive the assault. He also had to look over his shoulder to the west, as any sortie by the Italian battle fleet in support of the invasion would have to be countered. So, Cunningham made his deployments accordingly.

He formed four task forces, each led by one of his senior commanders. Force A, commanded by Vice Admiral Pridham-Wippell, was made up of the battleships *Queen Elizabeth* and *Barham*, escorted by five destroyers. It was to be deployed to the west of Crete, to intercept the Italians if they put to sea. Force B, led by Captain Rowley of the *Gloucester*, made up of *Fiji* and his own cruiser, plus two destroyers, would operate to the north, off the southern coast of the Peloponnese. It would cover the north-western approaches to Crete. Force C, under Rear Admiral King, with the AA cruisers *Dido* and *Coventry*, would cover north-east Crete, around the Kasos Strait. King's cruisers would be escorted by five destroyers. Finally, Force D, under the command of Rear Admiral Glennie, with *Dido*'s sister ships *Naiad* and *Phoebe*, accompanied by two destroyers, would patrol the western Aegean, between Piraeus (the port serving Athens) and the island of Antikythera, immediately north-west of Crete. If Glennie ran into trouble, Force B would be sent forward to support him.

With the German assault imminent, Cunningham ordered Pridham-Wippell's Force A to sail from Alexandria in the early evening of Wednesday 14 May. Force B would put to sea the following morning. That same day, Glennie's Force D put to sea, albeit without *Phoebe*, which due to a defect had to be replaced by the Australian cruiser *Perth*. Finally, Force C slipped out of Alexandria, bound for the Kasos Strait. Just in case, Cunningham organized a reserve naval group, Force A1, built around the battleships *Warspite* and *Valiant*, the light cruiser *Ajax* and eight destroyers. Cunningham turned his flagship *Warspite* over to Rear Admiral Rawlings, as he intended to command the coming battle from his headquarters in Alexandria.

These dispositions would not remain static. By necessity, the ships would have to return to Alexandria to refuel after a few days, and other cruisers were standing in readiness to reinforce these naval forces if required. As the days passed, Cunningham and his commanders would be forced to improvise, and respond to events. Fortunately, Cunningham was a commander who fostered initiative among his subordinates. A lot, though, depended on Cunningham's ability to respond to the enemy's moves when the invasion finally came.

Oberst Oskar Dinort commanded Sturzkampfgeschwader 2 'Immelman', an air corps equipped exclusively with the Ju 87 Stuka. His dive-bombers were responsible for many of the attacks on the Mediterranean Fleet during the campaign.

AXIS

In May 1941, both Adolf Hitler and the Oberkommando der Wehrmacht (OKW, the German Armed Forces High Command) were fully occupied finalizing the arrangements for Operation *Barbarossa*. It was scheduled to begin late the following month. The Balkan campaign had been fought primarily to safeguard the southern flank of this vast operation. Still, the success of the campaign, which culminated in the conquest of Greece, had encouraged the Luftwaffe to press for a continuation of the campaign, to capture Crete. That would safeguard Axis control of the Aegean basin, and would pose a threat to the Mediterranean Fleet, as its bombers could then dominate much of the eastern Mediterranean. Hitler acceded to the Luftwaffe, and so plans were drawn up for the invasion of the island. This invasion, codenamed Operation *Merkur* (*Mercury*), would primarily be a Luftwaffe affair. It would involve an airborne assault, in several waves, carried out under the aerial protection of the 716 fighters and bombers of VIII.Fliegerkorps. The airborne assault would be preceded by an extensive 'softening up' of the island's defences through repeated bombing attacks.

The paratroopers would be supported by troops from a mountain division, who would be transported to the island by boat, together with the Air Landing Division's heavier equipment and supplies, and also by air, after the Cretan airfields had been secured by the German paratroopers. The key element of the operation, though, was VIII.Fliegerkorps. Baron von Richthofen's aircraft had several tasks. The first of these was the 'softening up' attacks, to wear down the island's defences. Then, when the air assault came, their job was to protect the vulnerable transport planes as the paratroopers carried out their drops. With that done, the Fliegerkorps' bombers then had to support the paratroops, by carrying out numerous ground attack missions, at the behest of the commanders on the ground. They also had one other vital

Capitano di Corvetta Francesco Mimbelli (left) commanded the Italian torpedo boat RM *Lupo* during her clash with British surface forces to the north of Crete. His small warship, plus a handful of others, were the only vessels of the Regia Marina to support the invasion of the island. Next to him is Vice Admiral Förset, commanding Kriegsmarine forces in the Aegean.

mission. To prevent the Royal Navy from intercepting the Axis amphibious forces, bringing supplies, equipment and reinforcements to the island, they had to stop Cunningham's ships from intercepting the invasion convoys off the north coast of Crete.

This last mission was essentially a matter of sea denial. Traditionally, this was the task of another naval force, contesting the sea to prevent the enemy from operating effectively in it. This, on a larger scale, was exactly what Italian and German aircraft had been attempting in the Sicilian Narrows, between Sicily and the coast of Tunisia. The Axis aim there was to prevent Allied convoys from reaching Malta. Now, VIII.Fliegerkorps would carry out the same mission, concentrating its efforts around the two channels to the north-west of the island, between it and the Greek mainland, and in the Kasos Strait, to the north-east of Crete, between the island and the twin Italian-held islands of Scarpanto and Rhodes. Later, as the campaign evolved, the Luftwaffe would be called upon to range further out to sea, to the south of the island. This, though, was well within range of Richthofen's airfields in southern Greece.

Richthofen and his staff therefore had to divide their forces, in order to carry out these multiple missions. For the sea denial role, the task would fall primarily to reconnaissance aircraft, to pinpoint the presence of British naval forces. The attacks would then be carried out by the Sturzkampfgeschwader, the Fliegerkorps' air groups of dive-bombers. Some 150 of these Ju 87 Stukas would be earmarked for these maritime attack missions – roughly half of the dive-bomber force available to Richthofen. While they would be protected by fighters, Luftwaffe intelligence reports suggested that without *Formidable*, the threat posed by British aircraft in the area was minimal. So, the German dive-bombers would be able to carry out their attacks virtually unhindered, save for the defensive fire of the ships themselves.

The German airfields in the eastern Peloponnese were all less than an hour's flying time from Cape Spada on the north-west coast of Crete. Oberst Dinort's StG 2, based at Malaoi, whose Stuka air crews had been trained in anti-shipping operations, was fewer than 20 minutes flying time away from the cape. That meant Dinort's Stukas would be able to attack British warships in the Kythera Strait between the Peloponnese and Crete, and then return to base to refuel and rearm, before returning to the attack.

The effect would be that any enemy warship in the area would be subjected to a near-constant succession of air attacks, carried out by experienced pilots, who knew their business. In effect, they would turn the area into a naval killing ground. Because of this, Richthofen felt confident that the task of sea denial was fairly easy to accomplish. He believed his aircraft could effectively prevent the Royal Navy from passing through the Kythera Strait, or the Kasos Strait further east, to enter the Aegean Sea. So, in theory, the Axis reinforcement convoys should be safe from attack.

THE CAMPAIGN

THE PRELUDE

Admiral Cunningham's Mediterranean Fleet was ill prepared for the naval battle for Crete when it came. Its ships had been in action almost continuously for a month, they were short of stores and ammunition, and the crews were exhausted. Essentially, its ships and crews were already suffering from battle fatigue. The last thing the fleet needed was to be thrust into a fresh campaign, fought in waters dominated by the Luftwaffe. The reason for this lack of readiness can be traced back to 15 April 1941. That was when Cunningham, Wavell and Longmore, representing the three services, decided that they needed to draw up plans to evacuate the army from Greece. Three days later, the Greek Army was cut off in the Epirus Mountains, and soon faced collapse, while General Maitland Wilson's Commonwealth troops were being driven back into Attica. As the situation on the ground deteriorated, the evacuation, originally scheduled for 28 April, was hurriedly brought forward by four days.

Operation *Demon*, the codename for the evacuation of the army, was supervised by Vice Admiral Pridham-Wippell, based at Suda Bay in Crete, and assisted by Rear Admiral Baillie-Grohman in Athens. At their disposal

The deep-water anchorage of Suda Bay on the north coast of Crete was selected as a forward base by the Royal Navy, to be used as a springboard for operations in the Aegean. The deployment of the Luftwaffe in the region, though, rendered it impossible to operate from, or to defend.

The Italian battle fleet at sea on the eve of the Battle of Matapan. The Regia Marina could have intervened in the Crete campaign to add even greater pressure on Cunningham's fleet, but despite German urging, it avoided repeating its sortie of the previous month. The three cruisers on the left – *Zara, Pola* and *Fiume* – were all lost at Matapan.

was a hastily assembled force of cruisers, destroyers, makeshift troopships, infantry assault ships, landing craft and a number of smaller craft. As the Commonwealth troops straggled south, and communications with the army broke down, the evacuation became a hastily improvised affair, mainly carried out from beaches rather than ports. Three beaches near Athens and four more in the eastern Peloponnese were used, as well as the port of Piraeus. Local boats were commandeered by Baillie-Grohman, and gradually the men were taken to safety.

By day the Luftwaffe ruled the skies, and so the evacuations were carried out under cover of night. All ships were ordered to be away from the beaches by 0300hrs, so they had a chance to be well out to sea by daybreak. On the night of 24/25 April, over 12,000 men were embarked, followed by another 6,000 the following night. The third evening, 26/27 April, was the most successful, with over 21,000 men spirited to safety. By then the Germans had seized the Corinth Canal, and split southern Greece in two. Still, the following night almost 5,000 men were taken from the beaches in Attica, followed on 28/29 April by 5,400 from the Peloponnese, including General Freyberg and Baillie-Grohman. Smaller numbers were evacuated on the following two nights, as the Germans overran the Peloponnese, and the remaining Allied troops surrendered. Operation *Demon* was ended on 1 May. By then, though, over 50,000 troops had been evacuated.

It had been a harrowing operation, and losses had been heavy. Two destroyers, *Diamond* and *Wryneck*, were attacked and sunk by German Ju 88 bombers, while carrying 500 survivors from the troopship *Slamat*, which had succumbed to dive-bombers. All but 50 of the 1,000-strong soldiers and crew were lost. Apart from the *Slamat*, three other transports and five landing craft, and many of their evacuees, were killed. So, too, was the luxury yacht

Hellas, which was bombed in Piraeus and burned to the waterline before many of her 500 mostly civilian evacuees could escape. As well as the human and material cost, Operation *Demon* had also exposed the ships of the fleet to the full fury of the Luftwaffe. The crews had been subjected to daily attacks, and were exhausted from long spells at action stations. Worse, most of the ships had expended their AA ammunition, and there weren't enough shells in Alexandria to fully replenish them. So, many cruisers and destroyers began the Crete campaign with less than three-quarters of their ammunition.

There was little time to rest, though. A month before, on 1 April, Rommel had launched his offensive in North Africa, and by the time the evacuation from Crete was over, his tanks had reached the Egyptian frontier, and Tobruk was besieged. An Axis assault on Tobruk had been repulsed, but the situation in the Western Desert was still volatile. Worse, General Wavell's army had lost much of its equipment in Greece and Cyrenaica, and so was desperately short of materiel, especially tanks. A convoy was already en route to Egypt by way of the Cape of Good Hope, but Churchill ordered five fast ships to leave the convoy at Gibraltar and head directly to Alexandria. The ships carried 295 tanks and 53 fighters – equipment Wavell desperately needed. This operation was codenamed *Tiger*. Vice Admiral James Somerville's Force H escorted the *Tiger* convoy as far as Malta, where Cunningham's fleet would meet it, and escort it through the eastern Mediterranean.

There were other elements, too. Accompanying the convoy were reinforcements for Cunningham – the battleship *Queen Elizabeth* and the cruisers *Naiad* and *Fiji*. Heading west to Malta with Cunningham was another convoy of two tankers and four merchantmen, carrying much-needed ammunition and fuel to the beleaguered island. As the *Tiger* convoy passed through the Sicilian Channel on 8/9 May, a freighter struck two mines and sank, taking 57 tanks and 10 fighters down with her. The rest of the convoy was unscathed, and the following day it passed south of Malta to make its rendezvous with the Mediterranean Fleet. In reached Alexandria three days later. Similarly, the westbound Malta convoy also reached its destination without incident. As a result, Malta had been resupplied, and Wavell had enough tanks to plan Operation *Brevity*, a counter-offensive against Rommel. Operation *Tiger* had involved the bulk of Cunningham's fleet, and many of these ships had also seen action during Operation *Demon*. So, when they finally returned to Alexandria on 12 May, many of the worn-out ships' crews were hoping for a period of rest. As the First Lieutenant of the destroyer *Hotspur* put it: 'For months we had been working and fighting day and night. Perhaps one day a week in harbour, or rather one night of real sleep. We were tired and jaded. The physique of the ship's company was falling off. Even boats took a long time to hoist.' There would be no rest for them, though. Instead, these same weary ships' companies would be sent into action again, when the efforts demanded of them would be much greater. Many of those who survived the experience regard what came next as their most testing time of the entire war.

THE FLEET DEPLOYS

For some weeks now, Allied intelligence had suggested that the next Axis objective was Crete. For those willing to see, the island was practically

This view of the Leander-class light cruiser HMS *Orion* shows her HACS director, mounted on top of her forward superstructure, between the open bridge and the foremast. It was used to direct the fire of the cruiser's battery of 4in. HA (high-angle) AA guns.

indefensible, given the forces allocated to its defence. Crete was around 160 miles long and up to 35 miles wide, with a long mountainous spine running down its length. To the south of the mountains the ground and coast was largely rocky and inhospitable, but in the north the coastal plain was fertile, and fringed by beaches. Garrisoning it was an ad hoc collection of poorly equipped Commonwealth and Greek troops. Naturally, their commander Major-General Freyberg defended the north of the island, concentrating his forces on the coastal plain in the north-eastern part. There were also 5,300 Royal Marines there – part of the Mobile Naval Base Defence Organization (MNBDO) which was stationed at Suda Bay, with the intent of turning the anchorage into a useful forward base for the Mediterranean Fleet. The island's air cover was provided by a mixed bag of around 30 fighters, plus a few light bombers, and a small Fleet Air Arm contingent.

The real problem facing Admiral Cunningham, General Wavell and Air Chief Marshal Longmore was geography. In order to resupply or reinforce the garrison, ships had to sail there from Alexandria, and unload in Suda Bay or at the smaller port of Heraklion, both on Crete's northern coast. That meant the supply ships had to pass through the twin bottlenecks of the Kythera Strait to the west of the island, or the Kasos Strait to the east. Both were fairly easy to block using aircraft, submarines or surface forces. This supply route would certainly become unsustainable in the face of heavy air attacks from southern Greece. This meant that if reinforcements or supplies were brought in, they would have to be transported at night. This is what happened during the days before the invasion. On 15/16 May, *Gloucester* and *Fiji* transported a battalion of British infantry to Heraklion, while three nights later another was landed at Tymbaki on the island's southern coast.

To add to the problem, during early May the Axis had spread its hold throughout the Aegean, and the islands to the north of Crete were now in enemy hands. To the north-east, Rhodes and Scarpanto now boasted Italian air bases. In the event of a full-scale attack from sea and air, Crete would be extremely difficult to defend. As Cunningham himself succinctly put it: 'It would have suited us much better if the island could have been turned upside down.' The first German attacks began some 36 hours after Cunningham returned to Alexandria after the completion of Operation *Tiger*. Maleme and Heraklion were the initial targets. The intelligence reports reaching Cunningham included Ultra intercepts that suggested that the German invasion would begin on or soon after 15 May. This would be primarily an air assault, although some elements would also be sent to Crete by sea, and would be landed somewhere on the island's northern coast.

On Wednesday 14 May, as the first German dive-bombers began appearing over Crete, Cunningham ordered his fleet to sea. Pridham-Wippell's Force A was sent to the east of Crete, to guard against any intervention by the Regia Marina. He had two battleships under his command, protected by a screen of destroyers. Three smaller groups also followed the battleships to sea. Force C under King, with two cruisers and two destroyers, would position itself south of the Kasos Strait, where it could swoop in and attack any invasion convoy bound for Heraklion. Glennie's Force D, a similarly sized force of three cruisers and three destroyers, would cover Rethymnon, the small Venetian-built port in the centre of the island's north coast. Finally, Rowley's Force B

– two light cruisers – would patrol the waters around the Kythera Strait. They also had orders to land a battalion of infantry at Heraklion during their first sweep along the island's north coast.

The 4.7in./45 Mark XII QF ('quick-fire') gun in a twin mounting was carried in Tribal-class destroyers like HMS *Nubian*, and in J/K/N-class destroyers. It was capable of firing at aircraft as well as surface targets, and when combined with a HACS gunnery director, proved reasonably effective in throwing up a flak barrage in defence of a naval force.

In his orders, Cunningham made it clear that all three of the smaller forces would sweep the north side of the island at night, then retire to the south of Crete before dawn. By 15 May, these four naval groups were all in position. However, Ultra intercepts now revealed that the Luftwaffe had asked for a postponement of Operation *Mercury* until the morning of 20 May. It needed more time to assemble and organize the airborne troops, and to 'soften up' the island. This delay presented Cunningham with a fresh problem. His ships would have to return to Alexandria to refuel, and so, after repeated uneventful night sweeps, all four groups returned to port on 18 May. Cunningham planned to have them back in position by the time the rescheduled German air assault would begin.

Back in Alexandria, Cunningham had been holding a powerful force in reserve. Force A1, consisting of *Warspite* and *Valiant*, together with two light cruisers and several destroyers, was to be used to counter any unforeseen developments. So, too, was the aircraft carrier *Formidable*, which was waiting for more aircraft before she became fully operational again. Now, with Cunningham's other forces returning to port, it was time for him to send Force A1 to sea. So, Cunningham reluctantly gave up his flagship to Rear Admiral Rawlings, and shifted his flag into his headquarters ashore. The admiral would direct the rest of the campaign from there. Rawlings put to sea on the evening of 18 May, and by dawn on 20 May, he was in Pridham-Wippell's old position, 100 miles to the west of Crete. Intelligence reports, though, showed no indication that the Italian battle fleet intended to put to sea. Still, Force A and Force A1 were Cunningham's safeguard, in case these reports were wrong, or if the situation in Crete warranted the presence of battleships.

The German air offensive against Crete began on Wednesday 14 May, when the bombers of VIII.Fliegerkorps began bombing the Cretan airfields of

From 16 May on, Suda Bay was repeatedly bombed by the Luftwaffe. This shows the aftermath of an air attack on 18 May. In the centre, the wrecked heavy cruiser HMS *York* can be seen, crippled there by an Italian explosive motor boat attack on 26 March.

Maleme and Heraklion. German and Italian reconnaissance planes, based at Molaoi and Scarpanto respectively, also ranged far out to sea, looking for the British naval groups. Intelligence reports from Alexandria had reported their sailing, and so Richthofen was keen to locate and attack them before the main Cretan offensive began. The small convoy ASF 31 bound from Heraklion to Alexandria was located and attacked on the morning of 15 May, as it passed through the Kasos Strait. Seven Italian SM.79 bombers from 92 Gruppo based on Rhodes targeted the SS *Lossiemouth*, a merchantman with 2,000 non-combatants crammed on board. All the bombs missed, but it had been a close call. It also was a foretaste of what lay ahead.

On Friday 16 May, German bombers targeted the hospital ship *Aba* as she lay at anchor in Suda Bay. She was unscathed, and left that evening, bound for Haifa. She was attacked again the following afternoon, while passing through the Kasos Strait. This time the eight enemy aircraft were Stukas, but all their bombs missed. At 1730hrs, Force C arrived to escort her out of danger, but minutes later another eight Stukas appeared and attacked the ship. This time the fire from the AA cruiser *Coventry* and the light AA cruiser *Phoebe* drove them off, and the *Aba* only suffered minor damage from shrapnel, which killed one crewman and injured five more. On the *Coventry*, though, Petty Officer Alfred Sephton was mortally wounded when the cruiser was strafed, but he stayed at his post until the attackers had been driven off. He was posthumously awarded the Victoria Cross.

The attack on *Aba* in Suda Bay was part of a series of strikes on shipping there. Several British ships were damaged, including the already damaged and beached cruiser *York*, and the transport ship *Salvia*. The aim, of course, was to prevent the Allies from reinforcing or resupplying their garrison on Crete, before the airborne assault began. During these pre-invasion days, the RAF also managed to launch three of its own night-bombing raids by Bristol Blenheims of 30 and 203 squadrons, flying from North Africa. They targeted VIII.Fliegerkorps' airfields at Molaoi, Mycenae and Argos, but the raids achieved little, save for the boosting of British morale.

Meanwhile, the Luftwaffe air attacks on Crete continued, with the bombers protected by large numbers of fighters. The defenders did what they could to counter these attacks. Several German aircraft were shot down, but gradually the Allied air strength was worn away. On Monday 19 May, the decision was made to withdraw the few remaining RAF and Fleet Air Arm fighters from Crete, before the last of them were destroyed. This was a decision made with Cunningham's approval, even though it meant that his naval groups lost any form of fighter cover. So, by 20 May, when the German air assault began, there were no aircraft left to defend the island.

The Queen Elizabeth-class battleship *Warspite*, flagship of Admiral Cunningham, pictured berthed in Malta next to two D/E-class destroyers. During the Crete campaign, Cunningham turned his flagship over to his deputy, as he could exert better control over his scattered fleet from his headquarters in Alexandria.

To meet the threat, Cunningham took the opportunity of the need to refuel in order to reorganize his fleet. Force A1 had relieved Force A, which had temporarily returned to Alexandria. On the eve of the assault, Rear Admiral Rawlings was stationed 100nm to the west of Crete, with the battleships *Valiant* and *Warspite*, the cruiser *Ajax* and eight destroyers (*Decoy*, *Griffin*, *Hereward*, *Hero*, *Isis*, *Janus*, *Kimberley* and *Napier*). He had also been joined by the destroyers *Hotspur* and *Imperial*, which had been transferred from Force A. Rear Admiral King's Force C, consisting of the cruisers *Naiad* and *Perth* plus four destroyers (*Juno*, *Kandahar*, *Kingston* and *Nubian*) had refuelled, and were back on station to the south-east of Crete. Rear Admiral Glennie in the cruiser *Dido* was also back on station off south-western Crete, accompanied by the cruiser *Orion* and the destroyers *Greyhound* and *Hasty*.

Cunningham then ordered Rawlings to detach *Ajax*, *Hero* and *Hereward* to reinforce Glennie's Force D, which by nightfall was ordered forward to patrol the Kythera Strait. To the north-west of Crete Force B (the cruisers *Gloucester* and *Fiji*) had also returned to refuel, and was now heading back to its old patrol area, although it was now officially attached to Force A1. At dusk, King's Force C was also ordered forward to conduct a night sweep of the Kasos Strait. So, by the night of 19/20 May, all of Cunningham's forces were back on station, with two forces of cruisers and destroyers actively patrolling the seas at either end of the long island.

THE INVASION

The air assault on Crete began at 0800hrs on the morning of Tuesday 20 May. Heavy bombing raids on Maleme and around Suda Bay preceded large-scale parachute landings around Maleme and Prison Valley near Canea. Throughout the day, Richthofen's bombers and fighters were able to attack

Southern Aegean: the invasion of Crete, 20 May 1941

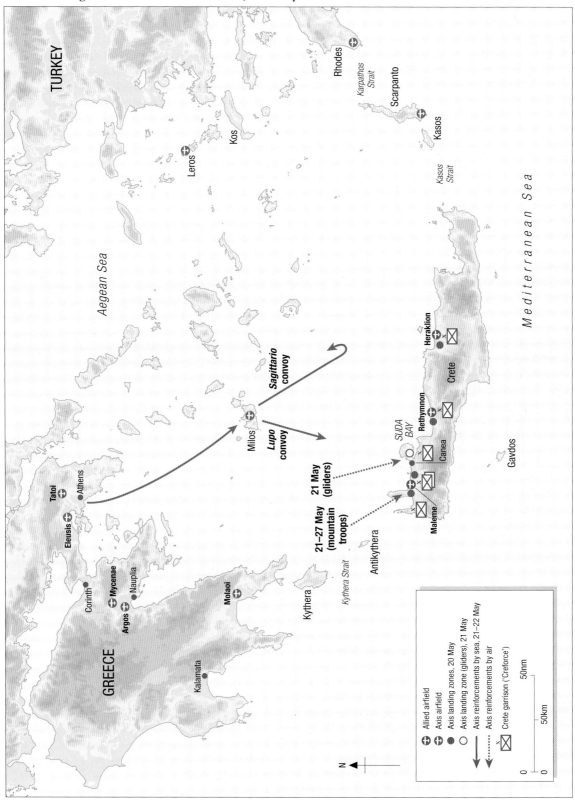

TURKEY

Rhodes

Karpathos Strait

Scarpanto

Kasos

Kasos Strait

Leros

Kos

Aegean Sea

Mediterranean Sea

Sagittario convoy

Milos

Lupo convoy

Heraklion

Crete

Rethymnon

SUDA BAY

Canea

21 May (gliders)

21–27 May (mountain troops)

Maleme

Gavdos

Tatoi

Athens

Eleusis

Antikythera

Corinth

Mycenae

Nauplia

Argos

Molaoi

Kythera

Kythera Strait

GREECE

Kalamata

Mediterranean Sea

N

Allied airfield

Axis airfield

Axis landing zones, 20 May

Axis landing zone (gliders), 21 May

Axis reinforcements by sea, 21–22 May

Axis reinforcements by air

Crete garrison ('Creforce')

0   50km

0   50nm

Allied defensive positions with relative impunity. The defenders fought back vigorously, and although the fighting continued throughout the day, the Germans made little headway. Later that afternoon, further landings took place to the east of Rethymnon, and around Heraklion. Again, though, the paratroopers were contained near their landing zones, and suffered heavy losses. Still, by nightfall over 3,000 German paratroops and glider troops had landed on the island. Their key objectives – the island's airfields – either remained held by the Allies, or in the case of Maleme had become a no man's land contested by both sides.

Word of the invasion reached Cunningham and his naval force commanders that morning. By that time, the night-time sweeps had been completed, and forces C and D had withdrawn to the south, before the enemy aircraft spotted them. Although the invasion was underway, there was little Cunningham could do to help the defenders until the following evening. So, they waited, although Cunningham ordered his forces to move closer to the island, but to remain out of sight of land. That day, all but Force A1 had been detected by German or Italian reconnaissance aircraft, but VIII.Fliegerkorps was fully committed to supporting the airborne invasion, and so was unable to attack. Finally, at 1800hrs, after receiving intelligence reports of possible invasion shipping in the Aegean, Cunningham ordered his commanders to close with the island, and issued his orders:

• Force B to conduct a night sweep to the south of the Peloponnese, before rendezvousing with Force A1 at a point 50 miles west of Crete at 0700hrs.

• Force C to pass through the Kasos Strait, then head east to sweep the northern coast of Crete to reach Heraklion at 0700hrs. For this sweep, it would be joined by the cruiser *Calcutta*.

• Force D to pass through the Kythera Strait, to sweep eastwards along the coast, to reach Canea by 0700hrs. The newly formed Force E, consisting of Captain Mack's 14th Destroyer Flotilla (*Ilex*, *Jervis* and *Nizam*), to conduct a night bombardment of Scarpanto airfield, then to withdraw southwards before dawn. The AA cruiser *Carlisle*, currently in Alexandria, to rendezvous with Force E at 0700hrs, at a point 50 miles east of Crete. Her task was to protect the destroyers from air attack.

A veteran German Fallschirmjäger emerging from a DFS 230 transport glider during the airborne invasion of Crete. While the majority of the first wave landed by parachute, a hundred gliders were also used, to transport both men and equipment.

Cunningham and his force commanders were aware of the airborne landings, but they lacked any hard information about them. It was hoped that the sweeps might produce more information, or even result in contact with an enemy amphibious force. In fact, all but one of the sweeps proved uneventful. The exception was King's Force C. Late that afternoon, it had been spotted by Italian reconnaissance aircraft flying from Rhodes. This was followed by an air attack by three SM.79 and four SM.84 torpedo bombers, but none of the torpedoes hit their targets. Force C entered the Kasos Strait without further incident shortly before nightfall, and steamed north at 20 knots.

King's ships were formed into two parallel columns, with *Kandahar* followed by *Perth* and then *Kingston* in line astern in the port column; and *Juno*, the flagship *Naiad* and then *Nubian* in the starboard one. Shortly after 2030hrs, lookouts on *Juno* spotted a number of small vessels 2 miles off their starboard beam. Moments later, they were identified as Italian MAS boats. These fast motor torpedo boats formed part of the 3rd MAS Flotilla, which was based on the island of Leros. When Force C was spotted that afternoon, three MAS 526- and two MAS 501-class boats were dispatched to attack the British as they passed through the strait.

So, the Italians had been waiting for the British, running slowly under auxiliary engines to reduce the risk of being spotted in the darkness. In theory, the Type 279 radar on *Naiad* should have detected them, but the small wooden-hulled boats didn't register on the radar display. In *Juno*, Commander John Tyrwhitt reacted quickly, and ordered full speed ahead. He tried to ram the nearest boat, *MAS 523*, but it managed to turn out of the way. *Naiad* and *Juno* promptly opened fire, at which point the Italian boats crash-started their engines and raced forward in between the two British columns. The boats then launched their torpedoes at a range of

When the Invasion of Crete began, Rear Admiral Glennie was ordered to lead Force D, made up of cruisers and destroyers, on a sweep to the north of the island. The aim was to intercept any attempt to invade Crete from the sea.

In the early hours of 26 March the heavy cruiser HMS *York* was attacked by six Italian MTB explosive torpedo boats in a daring raid on the British anchorage in Suda Bay. *York* was holed by two huge explosions, and had to be beached. The crippled ship was still there when the invasion of Crete began, and on 22 May *York* was scuttled to prevent her from falling into German hands.

Operations around the Kasos Strait, 20–22 May 1941

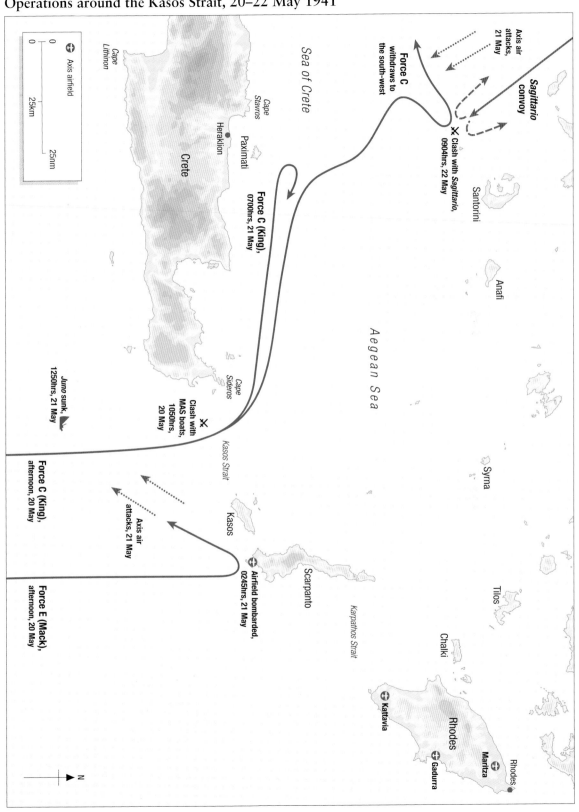

Sea of Crete

Cape Lithinon

Cape Stavros

Heraklion

Paximati

Crete

Force C (King), 0700hrs, 21 May

Juno sunk, 1250hrs, 21 May

Cape Sideros

Clash with MAS boats, 1050hrs, 20 May

Force C (King), afternoon, 20 May

Axis air attacks, 21 May

Force E (Mack), afternoon, 20 May

Kasos Strait

Kasos

Scarpanto

Airfield bombarded, 0245hrs, 21 May

Karpathos Strait

Aegean Sea

Syrna

Tilos

Chalki

Kattavia

Maritza

Gadurra

Rhodes

Rhodes

Axis air attacks, 21 May

Force C withdraws to the south-west

Sagittario convoy

Clash with Sagittario, 0904hrs, 22 May

Santorini

Anafi

Axis airfield

0   25nm
0   25km

N

39

German mountain troops preparing to embark on Ju 52 transport planes prior to their deployment in Crete. The Royal Navy's attacks on two troop convoys bound for Crete forced the Germans to airlift the bulk of these reinforcements to Crete by air.

550–650 yards. Amazingly, all ten torpedoes missed. Then the Italian boats raced off to the south-east, before shaping a course back towards Leros. It appears neither side managed to damage the other during this brief skirmish, apart from one MAS boat having its radio mast demolished.

After that, King's ships proceeded with even more caution, but the rest of the sweep proved uneventful. Reports had reached them that a number of small boats had been spotted off Heraklion, but when they got there, the sea was empty. The only other engagement that night took place off Scarpanto, when Captain Mack's three destroyers had briefly bombarded the airfield at 0245hrs, then set a course for the Kasos Strait, where he was ordered to rendezvous with King's Force C. Later that day, though, Mack's Force E was recalled to Alexandria. Dawn on Wednesday 21 May came at around 0530hrs. At that point, King ordered his force off Heraklion to withdraw eastwards to the Kasos Strait, which it reached without incident. He had also been joined by the AA cruiser *Calcutta*, as air attacks were now highly likely. By 0700hrs that morning, Rawlings' Force A1 was 60 miles to the west of Crete, steering south-west to rendezvous with Force D, which had completed its night sweep to Canea. Force B was also steaming south to join Rawlings.

Cunningham intended to move all of his ships well to the south of Crete during the day, to reduce their exposure to air attack. His plan was to wait there, and then to resume the night sweeps the following evening. Cunningham was not aware that Richthofen had already sent reconnaissance planes aloft that morning, with orders to find the British naval forces. Richthofen's Fliegerkorps was still heavily committed to providing air support to the embattled German airborne forces on Crete. That Wednesday, though, Richthofen had kept a significant portion of his squadrons in reserve, so they could be used to attack the British warships once they were detected. Some Stukas had also been moved to Scarpanto, to support the Italian air force in their efforts to cover the Kasos Strait. That day, the bulk of the German dive-bombers would be operating to the west of Crete. There, the British were about to learn a lesson in the effectiveness of air power.

THE FIRST CLASHES

One by one, all the British naval groups were detected. Then, Richthofen gave the order to attack. Force C was the first to suffer, at 1050hrs. It was a little way south of the Kasos Strait when the Regia Aeronautica bombers appeared, flying from Rhodes. In fact, they had tried to attack Force C earlier, but a heavy morning haze had cloaked the British ships. So, the three squadron-sized *gruppi* returned to refuel and try again. This time King's force was spotted by a Ro.43 scout plane 30 miles to the south-east of Crete, and the first of several attacks was carried out. These would continue intermittently for almost four hours. Force C was in the same formation as it had been the previous evening, except that *Calcutta* was now stationed between the two columns. The initial attack by 92 Gruppo's seven SM.79s was followed by other small-scale attacks by SM.84s, using a mixture of 250kg and 500kg bombs, as well as 45cm aerial torpedoes.

It seemed that King's ships led a charmed life, but a combination of a heavy AA barrage and good ship handling meant that all the bombs and torpedoes missed their targets. Then, at 1250hrs, King's luck ran out. This time the assailants were seven Z.1007bis 'Alcione' bombers from 50 Gruppo, based in Rhodes. These were level-bombers, and they dropped their ordnance from 3,000m as they passed over. *Calcutta*'s AA guns damaged two of the bombers, and other ships possibly hit other planes, but it was not enough to force the Italian pilots to turn away. Most of the 250kg bombs missed, but the stick dropped by Lieutenant Mario Morassutti's bomber landed squarely on the destroyer *Juno*. It was *Juno* which had tried to ram a MAS boat the previous evening. Commander Trywhitt's ship was torn apart by three direct hits, striking the destroyer from the bridge aft. She sank in less than two minutes, taking 116 of her crew down with her.

The destroyers *Kandahar*, *Kingston* and *Nubian* rescued 96 survivors, although five of these would die of their injuries before they reached

On the night of 21/22 May, Rear Admiral Glennie's Force D encountered a convoy of small transports bound for Maleme. In this depiction by Lieutenant-Commander Rowland Langmaid, *Dido*, followed by *Orion* and *Ajax*, are shown using their searchlights to pick out the transports, which were then sunk using 6in. guns.

Operations around the Kythera Strait, 21–22 May 1941

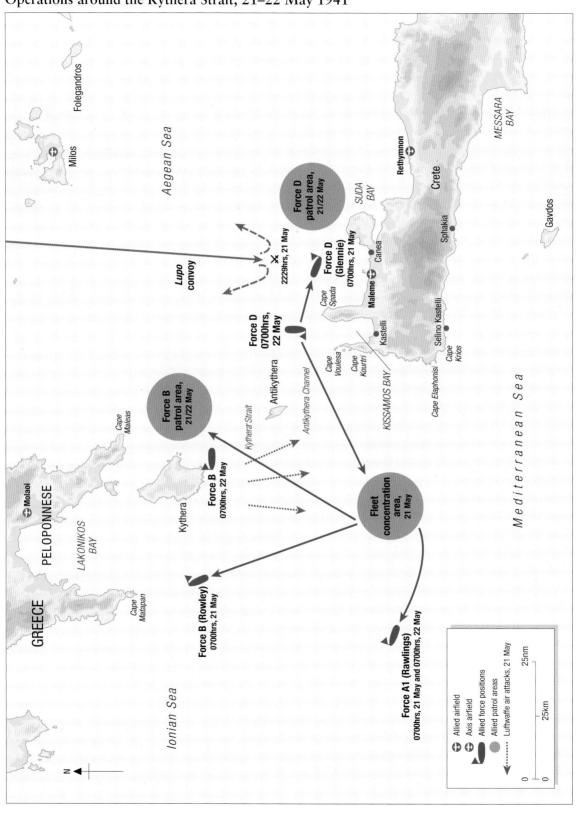

Folegandros

Milos

Rethymnon

Crete

MESSARA BAY

Aegean Sea

Force D patrol area, 21/22 May

SUDA BAY

Gavdos

Cape Spada

Force D (Glennie) 0700hrs, 21 May

Canea

Sphakia

Lupo convoy

2229hrs, 21 May

Maleme

Force D 0700hrs, 22 May

Antikythera

Kastelli

Selino Kastelli

Mediterranean Sea

Cape Voulesa

Cape Kourti

KISSAMOS BAY

Cape Krios

Antikythera Channel

Force B patrol area, 21/22 May

Cape Maleas

Kythera Strait

Cape Elaphonisi

PELOPONNESE

Moloai

Force B 0700hrs, 22 May

Kythera

Fleet concentration area, 21 May

LAKONIKOS BAY

GREECE

Cape Matapan

Force B (Rowley) 0700hrs, 21 May

Ionian Sea

N

Force A1 (Rawlings) 0700hrs, 21 May and 0700hrs, 22 May

Allied airfield
Axis airfield
Allied force positions
Allied patrol areas
Luftwaffe air attacks, 21 May

25nm

25km

Alexandria. One of the survivors, Petty Officer Lumley, recalled: 'Suddenly there was a blinding flash ... I have no recollection of any noise.' He jumped overboard, as it was clear the ship was sinking. He continued: 'Looking up from the water I could see the bows sliding under, and with no suction and hardly a ripple.' He was in the water for 20 minutes before he was pulled to safety by the crew of *Kandahar*. Afterwards, the pilot who sank *Juno* was known in the Regia Aeronautica as *Colpo Morassutti* ('Hit Morassutti'). This, though, was the penultimate attack. Following a final unsuccessful torpedo run at 1350hrs, the remainder of Force C was left alone.

The other British naval groups suffered, too. Force A1 was attacked in the late morning, this time by around 20 German level bombers, but no hits were scored, largely thanks to the heavy AA barrage thrown up by the warships. Having rendezvoused with Force B and Force D, Rawlings now had the advantage of having concentrated his AA firepower. He also benefited from the air search radar fitted to his battleships, which gave him some warning of impending attacks. The only damage inflicted during that forenoon was to *Ajax*, which suffered light splinter damage from a near miss.

There was a brief lull, but by 1320hrs the German bombers returned. The morning attacks had been carried out by a mixture of Ju 88s and Heinkel He 111s, but in the afternoon the main assailants were Stukas, most of which were operating from Molaoi in the Peloponnese. The attacks would continue at intervals throughout the afternoon, until shortly before 1600hrs. Then, after a lengthy gap, a last unsuccessful level-bomber attack was carried out against Force D at 1840hrs, after it was detached to carry out its night's sweep.

Rawlings' powerful battle fleet had survived the air assault – at least for the day. Now, though, he had two battleships, five cruisers and ten destroyers at his disposal. Unpleasant though the attacks had been, these British warships to the south-west of Crete were close enough to carry out another night sweep through the Kythera Strait once darkness had fallen. The only real problem facing Rawlings that afternoon was that his ships had expended most of their AA rounds during the course of the day. All they had to show for this was the shooting down of three Ju 88 bombers, although several other German bombers had been damaged. More importantly, if the attacks continued the following day, then the ships would potentially run out of the ammunition they needed to defend themselves.

HMS *Jervis*, a J/K/N-class destroyer, was the flagship of Captain Philip Mack, commander of the 14th Destroyer Flotilla, which was designated Force E during the campaign. *Jervis* and two other destroyers briefly bombarded the Axis airfield on Scarpanto (Karpathos) on 20–21 May.

THE *LUPO* CONVOY ACTION, 21 MAY 1941, 2229–2245HRS

On the evening of 21 May, Rear Admiral Glennie was ordered to conduct a sweep along the north coast of Crete, as far as Canea. Reports suggested the Germans would attempt to reinforce their airborne troops on Crete by sea, and a small convoy from the 1st Motor-Sailing Flotilla, consisting of 20 fishing caiques, small motor vessels and a pleasure craft, had indeed been sighted. They were escorted by the torpedo boat *Lupo*. After driving off the *Lupo*, Force D fell upon the convoy, and at least eight vessels were sunk.

CONDITIONS
Night action (2229hrs onwards)
Dawn at 0340hrs
Quarter moon
Sea state: Force 4 (choppy seas)
Wind: 24mph from south

D   1

E

4

A

F

B

⚓
MIMBELLI

C

REGIA MARINA
Capitano di Corvetta Francesco Mimbelli
1. *Lupo* (Spica-class torpedo boat – flagship)
2. German 1st Motor Sailing Flotilla: 20 vessels (15 fishing caiques, four small motor vessels, one pleasure boat) with 2,331 German mountain troops embarked. Course: 180° (south). Speed: 6 knots.

**CAPE SPADA
12NM TO SW**

Note: gridlines are shown at intervals of 1nm (1.85km)

2

5

10

1

2

FORCE D ⚓

GLENNIE

9

3

7

8

**CANEA
17.5NM TO SSE**

EVENTS

1. 2229hrs: *Janus* sights vessel ahead. Misidentification leads to the sighting not being reported.

2. 2234hrs: Lookouts on *Lupo* spot *Janus* off starboard beam, and she turns towards her. *Lupo* lays smoke to cover the convoy.

3. 2235hrs: *Lupo* sights *Dido* at a range of 1,200m (0.65nm).

4. 2235hrs: *Dido* opens fire on *Lupo*, followed by *Janus* and *Kimberley*.

5. 2236hrs: The convoy is ordered to scatter towards the north and east.

6. 2237hrs: *Lupo* fires two torpedoes at *Dido*, at range of 700m (0.38nm). These both pass astern of their target, between *Dido* and *Orion*.

7. 2240hrs: *Lupo* passes between *Dido* and *Orion*, then escapes towards the east.

8. 2240hrs: All the British ships are now firing at *Lupo*. Although hit over 18 times by 6in. shells, she avoids any serious damage.

9. 2244hrs: The British warships lose contact with *Lupo*, which escapes to the east-north-east.

10. 2245hrs: *Janus* sights the aftermost vessels in the convoy, and reports the sighting to Glennie. He in turn orders Force D to sink and destroy it. The British warships then break formation and ply the waters to the north for another four hours using searchlights to locate and sink the vessels of the convoy.

The Leander-class light cruiser *Orion* formed part of Rear Admiral Glennie's Force D, which eviscerated the *Lupo* convoy bound for Maleme, and then came under heavy air attack as she tried to extricate herself from the Aegean. *Orion* escaped with minimal damage, but was less fortunate a week later, when she was bombed in the Kasos Strait.

Meanwhile on Crete, the Germans had been bringing in reinforcements by Junkers transport planes, even though the only airfield they partially held, Maleme, was being swept by Allied artillery and machine-gun fire. Although casualties in planes and men were heavy, this airlift gave the Germans the strength they needed to gain control of the airfield. A night-time counter-attack by Commonwealth troops was repulsed, and the following morning more Junkers flew in, despite the airfield still being pounded by British artillery. These desperate measures provided a costly solution to Student's problem of securing a viable toehold on the island. However, reinforcements were also underway by sea. In Piraeus, Admiral Schuster had gathered together enough local fishing boats to transport a regiment of mountain troops to the island, plus their heavy weapons, ammunition and supplies. The plan was to land them near Maleme during the night.

The threat of a seaborne invasion was what had kept Cunningham's fleet in such dangerous waters throughout the day. The admiral intended to carry out another night sweep, once darkness had protected his ships from the Luftwaffe. Then, news reached him that confirmed his decision to sweep along the north coast was the right one. Early that afternoon, a Martin Maryland light bomber from 29 Squadron RAF left Egypt on a reconnaissance flight over the Aegean. Around 1630hrs, it spotted Schuster's flotilla of caiques 80 miles north of Crete, near the island of Milos. It appeared to consist of around 20 transport ships, escorted by a handful of small warships. Cunningham now had a target, and he issued his orders accordingly. Rear Admiral Glennie's Force D was to close with the land at dusk, heading for the Kythera Strait. Glennie would then sweep along the north coast as far as Canea, then return the way he had come. His primary task was to locate and destroy the enemy convoy.

Meanwhile, Captain Rowley's cruisers *Gloucester* and *Fiji*, supported by the destroyers *Griffin* and *Greyhound*, would cruise in the Kythera Strait that night, to prevent any enemy ships reaching Crete from the Peloponnese. Supporting them in turn would be Rear Admiral Rawlings' Force A1, which was still to the south-west of Crete. It would intervene if required. To the east of Crete, Force C was to return to the Kasos Strait under cover of darkness, then, like the previous night, probe the island's northern coast as far as Heraklion. If nothing were found, he would continue on towards the north, deeper into the Aegean. Clearly that would put his ships in great danger, as they would be heading even closer to the Axis airfields.

Fortunately for King, reinforcements had sailed from Alexandria that afternoon in the form of Captain Lord Louis Mountbatten's 5th Destroyer

Flotilla – his flagship *Kelly*, together with *Kashmir*, *Kelvin* and *Jackal*. They were due to join King off Crete at dawn the following morning. Similarly, the bulk of Captain Mack's 14th Destroyer Flotilla – formerly designated Force E (*Jervis*, *Nizam* and *Ilex*) had also left Alexandria, and were heading to reinforce King. Finally, Captain Waller's 10th Destroyer Flotilla (*Stuart*, *Voyager* and *Vendetta* – all Australian ships) were also on their way to join Rawlings off the western end of Crete.

Meanwhile, to the north, the grandly sounding 1st Motor Sailing Flotilla was on its way to Crete. This was the name given to the collection of commandeered caiques, small motor boats and other craft which had been gathered in Piraeus by Admiral Schuster, to move reinforcements and heavy equipment to Crete. On 19 May, a force of 2,331 mountain troops from 5.Gebirgs-Division had been embarked in 21 of these boats, and this convoy of small craft set off into the Aegean. Their first Italian escort – the torpedo boat *Sirio* – was damaged off Milos, so she was replaced by another, the *Curtatone*, which promptly struck a mine when leaving Piraeus. Finally, the Spica-class torpedo boat *Lupo* was given the task of escorting this makeshift convoy from Milos to Crete – a distance of just over 30 miles. It had been hoped to make the approach in daylight on 21 May, under a protective umbrella provided by the Luftwaffe. Now, though, the escort problems had delayed the venture. As the reinforcements were desperately needed on Crete, Schuster made the decision to continue on that evening, and planned to land the troops near Maleme under cover of darkness.

Glennie's Force D entered the Kythera Strait shortly before dark. The night was clear, and the seas calm. Both Glennie's flagship *Dido* and the cruisers *Ajax* and *Orion* were fitted with surface search radar, which greatly improved their chances of locating the convoy at night. The three cruisers were in line astern, with *Dido* in the lead, followed by *Orion* and *Ajax*. The destroyers were in line abreast, 500 yards ahead of the flagship, and spread out 1,000 yards apart from each other, with *Janus* at the northern end of the line. Once safely through the strait, Glennie's force headed due east at 20 knots. It was a dark night, with choppy seas and a strong wind from the south. Still, at 2229hrs, lookouts on *Janus* spotted a vessel off their port bow, about 2 miles ahead of them. Commander John Tothill increased speed and surged forward to investigate. It soon became clear that the vessel ahead of them was a small warship. It was the torpedo boat *Lupo*.

Four minutes later, a lookout standing next to Capitano di Corvetta (Lieutenant-Commander) Francesco Mimbelli on *Lupo*'s bridge spotted an enemy cruiser off their starboard bow. It was actually the *Janus*, streaking towards them out of the dark at 30 knots. By that time, she was about 1,300 yards away, and closing fast. Mimbelli immediately ordered his ship's two after torpedoes to be launched, but *Janus* turned abruptly, throwing off the torpedo team's aim. Instead, Mimbelli ordered his men to lay smoke, to screen the convoy astern of him. Otherwise he held his fire, as other destroyers loomed out of the dark behind *Janus*. Then, at 2235hrs, the Italians spotted *Dido*, heading straight towards them. Moments later the cruiser's 5.25in. guns opened up on *Lupo*, and the Italians responded by turning, launching their bow torpedoes at a range of 750 yards. *Dido* turned away to starboard to avoid them, as *Lupo* raced across her bows.

Then, *Orion* appeared, and joined in the firing as the *Lupo* curved back around the two cruisers, firing as she went. It was a spirited performance, but the torpedo boat's three 10cm guns were no match for Glennie's larger warships. The British ships were hitting *Lupo* now, so Mimbelli decided to break off the action. The British later claimed they had sunk the Italian warship, but she survived the action, and after returning to rescue what survivors she could find, she limped back into Piraeus. She had been hit 18 times, but many of the larger British shells had passed through her without exploding. Two men were killed, and another 25 wounded. As he withdrew, Mimbelli ordered the convoy to scatter. Much of the convoy escaped in the darkness, but the British warships still combed the area until 0300hrs on Thursday morning, hunting down and sinking as many of the small craft as they could. In the end they sank eight vessels from the convoy, and damaged several of the others, including the *Lupo*.

What saved many of the caiques was that the British shells simply went through their wooden hulls and superstructure without exploding. In a few cases the British resorted to ramming – the *Ajax* even damaged her bow when she rammed and sank a caique. Over 800 German soldiers had been carried on those ships, but many of them were rescued, either by the British or by other craft in the convoy. Official German records place their death toll at 324 officers and men. Most of these came from the 3.Bataillon of Gebirgs-Regiment 100. As for the British, the only casualties were on the *Orion*. She had been hit by 20mm Breda rounds fired by the *Lupo*, which killed two crew and wounded nine more. The cost, then, had been negligible, but Glennie must have been frustrated that so many vessels in the convoy had escaped in the dark. At 0300hrs, he gave the order to re-form into cruising formation, and Force D then headed back towards the comparative safety of the Kythera Strait.

The open bridge of the J/K/N-class destroyer *Kelvin*, pictured during a convoy operation in the Mediterranean. This open bridge arrangement gave Commander John Allison and his bridge crew an unobstructed view of what was happening around them, and made it possible to react quickly to dive-bombing attacks through fast manoeuvring.

THE LUFTWAFFE STRIKES

In the waters around Crete, dawn on Thursday 22 May came shortly after 0500hrs. At that moment, the British Mediterranean Fleet was still deployed in force in the waters to the north and west of Crete. Although this placed them in grave danger of heavy air attack, Admiral Cunningham thought the risk was worth taking if it meant the successful interception of all enemy reinforcements bound for Crete. Rear Admiral Rawlings' Force A1 was 45 miles

south-west of the Kythera Strait, while Rear Admiral Rowley's Force B was approaching the strait from the east, having patrolled there throughout the night, before sweeping as far east as Canea a few hours before dawn, at Cunningham's request. Rear Admiral King's Force C was to the north of Heraklion, having swept westwards along the coast from the Kasos Strait without making contact with anyone. Finally, Rear Admiral Glennie's Force D, after shooting up the *Lupo* convoy, was now approaching the Kythera Strait from the east. All of these naval groups were still well within range of VIII.Fliegerkorps.

During the night, Baron von Richthofen had learned of the British interception of the 1st Motor Sailing Flotilla, and was aware that several British naval groups were at sea to the north and west of Crete. As he put it in his war diary: 'By 0600hrs today reports have multiplied of British cruisers and destroyers in the sea areas north and west of Crete.' So, he changed his daily orders. While the bulk of VIII.Fliegerkorps would still provide close air support to Student's beleaguered German paratroopers on Crete, he diverted a sizeable portion of his force to hunt down and attack the British naval groups:

The Commonwealth light cruisers and destroyers deployed around Crete in May 1941 lacked the thick steel hull protection of larger warships. Machinery spaces, and the 'stokers' working in them, were vulnerable to near misses from bombs as well as from direct hits. The blast from them could buckle or pierce the hull plates, and cause flooding. It was therefore a dangerous place to be during an air attack.

Early on 22 May, the Italian Spica-class torpedo boat RM *Sagittario* took on Rear Admiral King's Force D, buying time for the convoy she was escorting to scatter. Despite the odds, Lieutenant Giuseppe Fulgosi and his crew attacked the British ships, then sped away in the confusion after suffering relatively minor damage.

- Oberst Rieckhoff's KG 2, with three *Gruppen* of Do 17s.
- Oberst Knust's LG 1, with two *Gruppen* of Ju 88s, and a third of He 111s.
- Oberst Dinort's StG 2, with three *Gruppen* of Ju 87s.
- Oberst Schalk's ZG 26 with two *Gruppen* of Me 110s.
- Major Woldenga's JG 77 with one *Gruppe* of Me 109s.

This meant that up to 462 German aircraft would be deployed against Cunningham's fleet that morning. Although the total number would be reduced slightly due to recent losses and aircraft under repair, up to 219 level bombers (108 Do 17s and 75 Ju 88 light bombers plus 36 He IIIs medium bombers), 108 dive-bombers (Ju 87 Stukas), 135 fighters (90 Me 110s and 45 Me 109s) would take part in these naval strikes. In addition, at least two squadrons of reconnaissance aircraft were ordered to take off before dawn, to pinpoint the British ships, and to direct the bomber groups towards their targets. By then, though, Richthofen had a fair idea where the various British naval forces were to the west of Crete, and so that was where the reconnaissance efforts were concentrated. The result was the appreciation of the situation and British dispositions that Richthofen wrote about at 0600hrs that morning.

LG 1 and KG 2 were based at Eleusis and Tatoi near Athens, 100 miles and 40 minutes' flying time from the island of Antikythera, in the centre of the Kythera Strait. ZG 26 was at Argos in the Peloponnese, roughly the same distance from the strait, but only 20 minutes in a twin-engined fighter. The III Gruppe of JG 77 with its Me 109s operated from Molaoi, ten minutes away from the strait. Meanwhile, Dinort's StG 2 was now divided, with two *Gruppen* based at Mycenae and Molaoi in the Peloponnese, 100 miles and 50 miles respectively from the strait. By using Molaoi as a forward base for both Stuka *Gruppen*, Dinort's dive-bombers could be over Antikythera in just 30 minutes. His third *Gruppe*, commanded by Captain Brücker, had been sent to the Italian-occupied island of Scarpanto. It was just 40 miles or 20 minutes' flying time from the Kasos Strait, but 180 miles or 95 minutes from the Kythera Strait. Dinort felt confident, though, that with a bit of hasty planning, all three *Gruppen* could refuel and rearm at Molaoi if the need arose. This, of course, meant that the same squadrons could make several sorties over the duration of the day.

Meanwhile, off Heraklion, King had received intelligence reports that a second enemy convoy was approaching Crete from the north, and was probably bound for Heraklion. So, in line with Cunningham's new orders, he continued his sweep towards the north-west at 20 knots, heading deeper into the Aegean, and therefore closer to the enemy airfields. To make things worse, the rough seas and low cloud of the night had dissipated, leaving much calmer seas and clear skies. So, it was with some trepidation that King continued his sweep towards the north-west. To extend his search radius he had to spread his destroyers out in line abreast, which naturally meant they were less able to defend each other if attacked from the air. King's ships were deployed in a T-shape, with the destroyers in extended line abreast ahead of him, and his cruisers (*Naiad*, *Perth*, *Calcutta* and *Carlisle*) in line astern behind his flagship, with *Naiad* stationed 1,000 yards behind the destroyers.

It was King's force which would attract the brunt of the Luftwaffe's attention that morning, following detection by Richthofen's reconnaissance aircraft. The first wave, a squadron of 12 Ju 88 light bombers from LG 1's I Gruppe, appeared over the British ships just after 0700hrs. Although no ships were hit, the defenders wasted precious AA ammunition trying to fend off the attack. The air attacks would continue throughout the morning, and for the most part these would be carried out by the Ju 88s of LG 1, or the Do 17s of KG 2, flying from their airfields near Athens. It was during these frequent squadron-sized attacks that King's ships first made contact with the enemy convoy.

Earlier that morning, the 2nd Motor Sailing Flotilla had left the Aegean island of Milos, and began the 70-mile journey to Crete. Like the first convoy, it was made up of caiques, small motor boats and small coasters – 30 of them in all. Embarked in them were 4,000 German mountain troops. Its only escort was the Italian Spica-class torpedo boat *Sagittario*, under the command of Lieutenant Giuseppe Fulgosi. The convoy headed due south, making 6 knots. Then, at 0830hrs, a radio message from Admiral Schuster ordered them to turn around and head back to Milos. The German admiral knew that British light forces were in the area, and after the attack on the *Lupo* convoy he was taking no chances. They were roughly 30 miles south of Milos when Fulgosi ordered the convoy to turn around.

A near-miss from an Italian bomb – the Dido-class AA cruiser HMS *Naiad* under attack in the Kasos Strait on 21 May. The following day, Rear Admiral King's flagship was badly damaged while heading for the Kythera Strait, after engaging the *Lupo* convoy.

THE *SAGITTARIO* ACTION, 22 MAY 1941 (PP. 52–53)

During the night of 21/22 May, Rear Admiral King's Force C patrolled to the north of Crete, searching for a reported enemy troop convoy. This was made up of 30 small fishing vessels and motor boats, hastily commandeered as troop transports, and escorted by a single Italian motor torpedo boat, the *Sagittario*. At 0847hrs, *Sagittario* was sighted by a British destroyer. The convoy had already turned away, but Lieutenant Fulgosi of the *Sagittario* needed to buy time to let it escape. After laying smoke, he steamed towards the British and opened fire. As King had four cruisers and three destroyers this seemed suicidal, but by zig-zagging at high speed the *Sagittario* avoided any serious damage. She even managed to hit the British destroyer *Kingston* and launch torpedoes at the enemy cruisers before making her escape.

This scene shows *Sagittario* (**1**) engaging the destroyer *Kingston* (**2**), while two of King's cruisers, *Naiad* (**3**) and *Perth* (out of view, to the left), fire at the speeding *Sagittario*. The destroyer *Nubian* (**4**) can be seen engaging stragglers from the convoy desperately seeking to disappear within a smokescreen (**5**). In the end, thanks to Fulgosi's bravery, only two of the small transports were caught and sunk by Force C.

Around the same time, a dozen miles to the south-east, lookouts on *Perth* sighted a single caique – a straggler from the *Lupo* convoy. The cruiser was detached and headed off to sink it, while the rest of Force C continued on its way. Although the intermittent air attacks continued, King pressed on, and at 0847hrs he was rewarded with another sighting – this time a lone Italian torpedo boat. Fulgosi spotted the smoke of the approaching British ships, too, and ordered his convoy to disperse. To protect his charges, Fulgosi turned the *Sagittario* around and closed with the enemy, while making smoke. King ordered his destroyers to pursue the convoy, while his cruisers concentrated on the approaching escort. At 0904hrs *Sagittario* opened fire on the destroyer *Kingston* at a range of 6½ miles, and the British destroyer fired back. When the range closed to 5½ miles the British cruisers opened fire, forcing Fulgosi to zigzag. However, his gunners still managed to score a hit on *Kingston*'s bridge with one of their three 10cm guns.

When the range dropped to 4 miles, Fulgosi launched a spread of four torpedoes at the cruisers, before making more smoke and turning away. The torpedo salvo missed, despite later Italian claims that *Naiad* had been hit. In fact, the British ships were under air attack at the time, and the smoke the *Sagittario*'s crews saw came from a minor bomb hit. Meanwhile, *Kingston* claimed two hits on *Sagittario*, and after spotting part of the rapidly dispersing convoy through the smoke, Lieutenant-Commander Philip Somerville ordered his destroyer's guns to switch targets to the caiques. At least two of them were sunk by her 4.7in. shells. Meanwhile, *Sagittario* made good her escape.

By now the time was 0928hrs. Although a few small caiques had been spotted, King was still unaware that he had made contact with a large convoy. They were now just 25 miles south of Milos, and every minute took Force C further into danger. The air attacks were getting heavier, too, and his ships were quickly running out of ammunition. So, King gave the order to break off the action. He was now roughly the same distance from the Kasos Strait (by which he had entered the Aegean Sea) and the Kythera Strait. Either way, with his speed limited to 20 knots thanks to damage to *Carlisle*'s engines, it would take him about four hours to round the end of Crete and head south towards safer waters. He opted to head south-west, towards Antikythera, and the protection of Rawlings' battle fleet.

As a result, the bulk of the *Sagittario* convoy escaped. Afterwards, King was criticized by both Cunningham and Churchill. The fleet commander argued that the destruction of the convoy would have warranted the sacrifice of part of Force C. He even suggested that when faced with air attack, King's safest place would be in the midst of the convoy. This, though, was not really true. Later, Fulgosi reported that the battered *Sagittario* had been attacked five times by German bombers as the convoy withdrew. Churchill also dryly commented that this withdrawal did not save Force C from air attack. This was true – they still had to run the gauntlet of Luftwaffe air attacks – but it was also unfair, as any further delay in retiring would have invited the complete destruction of King's force. For his part, when *Sagittario* returned to Piraeus, Lieutenant Fulgosi was fêted by the German mountain troops, whose lives he had undoubtedly saved.

As King's Force C headed towards the south-west, its progress was tracked by Luftwaffe reconnaissance planes. By then, though, his ships had regrouped after the pursuit of the convoy, and were now concentrated, to

The G/H/I-class destroyer HMS *Griffin* commanded by Lieutenant-Commander John Lee-Barber formed part of Force B during the initial operations around Crete. *Griffin* was the only warship of the force to survive the debacle of 'Black Thursday'.

provide a more potent AA defence. In these situations, there definitely was safety in numbers. It was just as well, as the air attacks proved relentless. For the Luftwaffe, the situation simply could not be better. Several groups of British warships now lay within easy reach of their airfields.

That day, any attempt to attack in whole air groups or even squadrons quickly gave way to a simpler system. After a bombing run, the bomber would return to a friendly airfield – ideally one nearby – where the aircraft would refuel and rearm. It would then return to the fray. This meant that attacks were made in smaller flight-sized groups. The effect was even more debilitating for the British. With near constant air attacks, the crews had to remain at Action Stations for hours on end, and were subjected to near-constant pressure. It also meant the British were almost constantly using up their ammunition by throwing up flak barrages with their heavier AA guns. Eventually, they would begin to run out, which would leave the ships defenceless.

BLACK THURSDAY

Rear Admiral King's Force C was not the only British naval group to be attacked that morning. To the south-west was Captain Rowley's smaller Force B, consisting of his own cruiser *Gloucester*, accompanied by *Fiji* and the destroyers *Greyhound* and *Griffin*. At dawn, it was heading east at 20 knots, having patrolled as far as a point 25 miles north of Canea without incident. It had been located by the Luftwaffe shortly before dawn, and the first wave of StG 2's Stukas arrived shortly after 0630hrs. Rowley's four warships were subjected to a series of intermittent air attacks which would last for 90 minutes. Both StG 2's Ju 87s and LG 1's Ju 88 level bombers were involved in these attacks, and while initially squadron-sized formations were used, by the end the attacks were being made by smaller formations. The last of the bombers flew off at 0803hrs, as Force B had completed its passage of the Kythera Strait.

This time, Rowley had been lucky. Both light cruisers had suffered only minor damage – underwater concussion from near misses buckled some hull plates on *Gloucester*, while *Fiji* had parts of her superstructure riddled by splinters from bombs fragmenting close to the ship. However, this had knocked out *Fiji*'s HACS AA gun director, which significantly detracted from her ability to fire an effective flak barrage. Both destroyers emerged unscathed. By the end of these attacks, though, both cruisers were dangerously short of AA ammunition. *Fiji* was down to 30 per cent, while *Gloucester* had just 18 per cent of her 4in. dual-purpose shells left. When these last shells ran out, the cruisers would be virtually defenceless.

All British cruisers and destroyers which took part in the Crete campaign had open bridges. It was from here that the Commanding Officer would 'fight' his ship during an air attack, where he could, in theory, see the bombers make their attacks, and so con his ship to avoid them. It also rendered the bridge staff vulnerable to splinter damage or strafing attacks. This shows the bridge of a Town-class light cruiser, similar to *Gloucester*.

Meanwhile, Rear Admiral Glennie's Force D (the cruisers *Dido*, *Orion* and *Ajax*, and the destroyers *Hasty*, *Hereward*, *Janus* and *Kimberley*) were some way ahead of them, having passed through the Kythera Strait shortly after dawn that morning. At 0700hrs, it rendezvoused with Rawlings' battle fleet 45 miles to the south-west of Antikythera. After welcoming Glennie by signal, Rawlings requested a report of his AA ammunition stocks. The news was not good – the three cruisers were down to between 25 and 40 per cent, with Glennie's flagship *Dido* having the least. When the report was passed to Cunningham, he ordered Glennie's ships to return to Alexandria for replenishment. Due to the threat from the Luftwaffe, though, Rawlings only released Force D at 1045hrs.

So, throughout the forenoon, Rawlings' Force A1, accompanied by Force D and eventually Force B, remained in position to the south-west of Antikythera, where it would be in a position to assist King's beleaguered Force C if required. As Rawlings described it in his report, his ships were, 'serving a useful purpose attracting enemy aircraft'. Fortunately for the British, these attacks were both sporadic and poorly coordinated. By concentrating his forces, Rawlings was giving his ships the best possible chance to defend themselves through mutual support. Then, at 1225hrs, a radio message arrived which would change the whole situation. It was from King, reporting that he was under heavy air attack, that his flagship *Naiad* had been damaged, and that Force C was in urgent need of support. So, Rawlings ordered the battle fleet to increase speed to 23 knots, and to steam towards the Kythera Strait, where he hoped to rendezvous with King.

The air attacks on Force C had resumed shortly after 1000hrs. This time his assailants were all level bombers, Ju 88s from Gruppe I of LG 1 and Do 17s from KG 2. These twin-engined bombers carried four 250kg bombs apiece (or up to five bombs in the Ju 88s), and so although the attacks were

poorly coordinated, and mostly carried out by small flight-sized groups of aircraft, they were highly dangerous. In just one ten-minute period, from 1115 to 1125hrs, *Naiad* reported 36 near misses. Even these caused damage, as hull plates buckled under the repeated blasts, and flooding was reported in several compartments, including her engine room. This led to her speed being reduced to 17 knots. Just as seriously, splinters from the exploding near misses peppered her superstructure, and put two of her four twin 5.25in. AA turrets out of action.

King's other three cruisers were also bombed heavily. Both *Perth* and *Calcutta* managed to avoid any serious damage thanks to some skilled high-speed manoeuvering, but *Carlisle* suffered a direct hit on her forward superstructure which wrecked the bridge and killed most of the bridge crew, including the cruiser's commanding officer, Captain Thomas Hampton. The fire that resulted was eventually extinguished, and the cruiser kept on fighting. Once more, the Luftwaffe concentrated on the cruisers, so Force C's four destroyers were spared the worst of the attacks. Meanwhile, a few miles to the east, as Rawlings' Force A1 approached the entrance to the Aegean, it, too, came under increasingly heavy air attack. This was to be expected, but it reinforced the point that they were sailing into danger.

On Rawlings' flagship *Warspite*, the battleship's lookouts could see where King's ships were before any vessels were spotted. At 1312hrs, their location was marked by the AA bursts in the sky above them. It took another ten minutes before the ships themselves could be seen, with two of them trailing smoke. The two forces closed with each other at a combined rate of 40

knots, and so by 1335hrs they had joined each other, with the battle fleet assuming its position immediately astern and around the flanks of King's battered cruisers. For the first time that day the British forces were fully concentrated, and so in theory they were better able to defend themselves. The drawback, of course, was that VIII.Fliegerkorps would throw everything they had against the British battle fleet.

These attacks began the moment the two forces converged. At 1332hrs, as *Warspite* was manoeuvering into position astern of King, a flight of three Me 109 fighters from III./JG 77 swooped towards the battleship, one behind the other. Clearly, the fighter pilots were not going to be left out, as each of the Messerschmitts carried a 250kg bomb beneath their fuselage. They released their bombs at a height of 150m, and although Captain Fisher turned the battleship hard to port, it was not enough. One bomb narrowly missed *Warspite*'s starboard side, and a second landed in front of her. The third bomb, though, struck the battleship's upper deck, just in front of the starboard 4in. AA battery. The bomb penetrated the lightly armoured foredeck, only to ricochet off the armoured deck beneath it and then explode. It blew the forward twin 4in. mounting overboard, and damaged the adjacent one. Four starboard 6in. guns were also put out of action, a 90ft gash was ripped in the foredeck, and a 50ft hole ripped in the ship's side. Fires burned fiercely.

Warspite's First Lieutenant, Commander Charles Madden, led a damage control team to the starboard 6in. battery deck, where he found scores of dead and wounded men. Before they could be tended, his team had to put out the fire ranging inside the casemate. While he was seeing to the wounded, he glanced through a hole in the deck above him, to see more waves of aircraft approaching. In all, *Warspite* lost 69 casualties, 38 of which were killed, and the rest wounded. It was the first serious damage *Warspite* had suffered since

HMS *Kipling* returning to Alexandria on 24 May, with the survivors from *Fiji* on board. The destroyer ran out of fuel 50nm from her destination, and had to be towed into port. Her actions warranted Lieutenant-Commander Aubry St Clair-Ford and his crew being cheered into port by the rest of the fleet.

HMS *Gloucester* under attack, as photographed by a Luftwaffe airman on 22 May. A near miss from a large bomb can be seen off the cruiser's port beam, as Captain Henry Rowley manoeuvres to avoid being hit. He could not avoid them all, though, and at 1527hrs *Gloucester* was hit – the first of several bombs that crippled and sank the ship.

the Battle of Jutland, a quarter of a century earlier. Although most of her starboard guns were now out of action, *Warspite* successfully avoided being hit again, despite being attacked over a dozen times. This was particularly impressive, as her starboard AA batteries had now effectively been put out of action.

At roughly the same moment as the bomb struck, *Naiad* flashed a message to *Warspite*, informing Rear Admiral Rawlings that Rear Admiral King was assuming active command of the battle fleet. Officially, King was senior to Rawlings, having reached flag rank in 1938, over two years before Force A1's commander. Rawlings would retain command of Force A1, but King would be in overall command of the whole battle fleet. This was unfortunate in two ways. First, unless it was unavoidable, it was usually unwise to change command of a force while it was under attack. Secondly, when he assumed command, King had no idea about the combat effectiveness of Force A1 and Force B, especially their ammunition stocks. For the moment, King was more concerned in fending off the seemingly continual air attacks on his ships, and extricating them from danger, than asking for ammunition reports. This, though, would become a critically important factor in what followed.

Amid all the drama of these few moments, the destroyer *Greyhound* had been momentarily overlooked. At 1315hrs, as the two forces steamed towards each other, a large caique was spotted to the north of Antikythera. Suspecting she was part of the scattered *Lupo* convoy, at 1320hrs Rawlings detached *Greyhound* to close in and sink her. She sank her target a few miles north of Antikythera, then at 1351hrs she turned to rejoin the rest of the fleet. It was then that she was spotted by a group of eight Stukas from StG 2. They turned to attack, and Commander Walter Marshall-A'Deane tried unsuccessfully to evade all of the bombs. At least two of the 250kg bombs struck the destroyer, one amidships and one or two aft. She began sinking by the stern, and the crew started abandoning ship. Her gun crews, though, stood by their AA weapons as long as they could, to protect their shipmates.

Several miles to the south-east, Rear Admiral King saw what had happened, and detached the destroyers *Kandahar* and *Kipling* to pick up *Greyhound*'s survivors. Then, at 1402hrs, almost as an afterthought, he ordered *Gloucester* and *Fiji* to join the two destroyers, to provide AA protection for them. King was unaware how low the AA ammunition stocks on the two cruisers had become. What he should have realized, though, was that by dividing his force, he was not only weakening its overall AA defence, but he was placing these four warships in the gravest danger. Meanwhile the bulk of the fleet continued to steam away towards the south-west, its speed limited to 18 knots due to the damage suffered by *Warspite*. Meanwhile, her sister ship *Valiant* had so far avoided any real damage, although she had been showered by splinters from near misses.

Almost immediately, the two groups of rescue ships came under fierce air attack from both dive-bombers and level bombers. Meanwhile, *Greyhound* had finally sunk, 15 minutes after she was hit, and the survivors bobbed in the water close to her one surviving boat. When *Kandahar* and *Kipling* approached, they lowered their own boats, then veered away at speed to avoid the bombs which were now directed at them. Both destroyers dodged any direct hits, but *Kipling* suffered minor damage from three near misses. *Kipling*, though, was now among the survivors, floating some 5 miles west of the small islet of Pori, and 7 miles to the north-west of Antikythera. The rescue mission did not go well. Passing German aircraft strafed the boats, and killed dozens of men in the water. Eventually, the survivor-laden boats were recovered by the two destroyers, while still under heavy air attack.

At 1456hrs, a signal from King ordered them, at their discretion, to rejoin the rest of the battle fleet. So, after dropping a dozen Carley floats and leaving two boats behind to aid the men still in the water, the two destroyers sped away to the south. In the end, 80 men from *Greyhound*'s crew were lost, and 63 rescued. Four more were captured by the Germans. While these survivors owed their lives to the efforts of the crews of *Kandahar* and *Kipling*, their safety was still far from assured, as the destroyers continued to be targeted by enemy bombers. Most of the German aircraft, though, ignored them in order to concentrate on the larger and more prestigious targets to the south. Two of these were now approaching the destroyers; *Fiji* was closing with them fast, while *Gloucester* was a mile astern of her.

Meanwhile, the main battle fleet was still being subjected to relentless and heavy air attacks. At 1413hrs, King in *Naiad* signaled Rawlings in *Warspite* requesting closer support for Force C, as his ships were almost completely out of AA ammunition. Rawlings did what he could, although by now he was becoming increasingly concerned about Rowley's reinforced Force B to the north. He shared his concerns with King by signal, and told him just how low ammunition stocks were in Rowley's two cruisers. Twelve miles to the north, when *Fiji* and *Gloucester* reached the two destroyers, Captain Rowley of the *Gloucester* assumed command of the force. At that moment, he received a signal from King ordering him to withdraw at his discretion, together with any ships in company. With that, Rowley formed his small independent force so they could better protect themselves against air attacks, and then ordered his ships southwards towards the battle fleet.

At 1530hrs, lookouts on *Naiad* reported that *Fiji* and *Gloucester* were approaching from the north, accompanied by two destroyers. King was hugely relieved, but became concerned when he noticed how *Gloucester* was wreathed in smoke. He then saw that Rowley's ships were being subjected to a series of dive-bomber attacks. Their AA barrage also appeared weak, which suggested they were almost out of ammunition. The smoke pouring from *Gloucester* was the result of two 250kg bombs, which struck the ship at 1527hrs. One exploded outside the gunroom and damaged a boiler room, the electrical generator and the radio room, while the second hit the base of the foremast, wrecking the HACS director. Fires sprang up in several places. At the same time, the cruiser was subjected to a string of near misses, which damaged her hull below the waterline and caused flooding. As a result, the cruiser was now stripped of power to her guns, and the fire control system she needed to fire them effectively.

As the *Gloucester*'s speed dropped due to the damage to her boilers, she suffered a string of other blows. The fire led to an explosion beside the port-side torpedo tubes, but fortunately Captain Rowley had ordered the

VIII
RICHTHOFEN

Note: gridlines are shown at intervals of 15nm (27.8km)

MOLAOI AIRFIELD

CAPE MALEAS

PELOPONNESE

LAKONIKOS' BAY

ELAFONISOS

KYTHERA

8

KYTHERA

CAPE MATAPAN

CONDITIONS
Daylight action
Sea state: Force 2 (slight swell)
Wind: 16mph from south

1

A

IONIAN

FORCE A1
RAWLINGS

FORCE B
ROWLEY

FORCE C
KING

LUFTWAFFE
FLIEGERKORPS VIII (GENERAL DER FLIEGER VON RICHTHOFEN, BASED IN ATHENS)
Kampfgeschwader (KG) 2 (Oberst Reikoff) – operating from Tatoi near Athens
Three air groups: I./KG 2, II./KG 2, III./KG 2, each with 36 Do 17 Z2 light bombers
Lehrgeschwader (LG) 1 (Oberst Knust) – operating from Eleusis near Athens
Two air groups: I./LG 1, III./LG 1, each with 36 Ju 88 A5 light bombers
One air group: II./LG 1, with 36 He 111 H3 medium bombers
Sturzkampfgeschwader (StG) 2 (Oberst Dinort) – operating from Mycenae and Molaoi in the Peloponnese
Two air groups: I./StG 2, II./StG 2, each with 36 Ju 87 R2 Stuka dive-bombers
Zerstörergeschwader (ZG) 26 (Oberst Schalk) – operating from Argos in the Peloponnese
One air group: (II./ZG 26), with 45 Me 110 C4 heavy fighters
Jadgeschwader (JG) 77 (Major Woldenga) – operating from Molaoi in the Peloponnese
One air group: II./ZG 26, with 45 Me 109 F2 fighters

On the morning of 22 May, the Mediterranean Fleet was scattered, with forces to the east, north and west of Crete. A fourth group, Rear Admiral King's Force C, was still in the Aegean, and under heavy air attack. When King requested Rawlings' support, Force A1 entered the Kythera Strait to provide what help it could. The two forces combined at 1335hrs, and soon came under heavy air attack.

AEGEAN SEA

CAPE SPADA

KISSAMOS BAY

PORI

CAPE VOUSKA

ANTIKYTHERA

ANTIKYTHERA CHANNEL

CRETE

6

B

5

4

3

10

9

ROYAL NAVY
MEDITERRANEAN FLEET (ADMIRAL CUNNINGHAM, BASED IN ALEXANDRIA)

A. Force A1 (Rear Admiral Rawlings)
Warspite (flagship, Queen Elizabeth-class battleship)
Valiant (Queen Elizabeth-class battleship)
Napier (J/K/N-class destroyer)
Decoy (D/E-class destroyer)
Hero (G/H/I-class destroyer)
Hotspur (G/H/I-class destroyer)

B. Force B (Captain Rowley) – now attached to Force A1
Gloucester (flagship, Gloucester-class light cruiser)
Fiji (Fiji-class light cruiser)
Griffin (G/H/I-class destroyer)
Greyhound (G/H/I-class destroyer)

C. Force C (Rear Admiral King)
Naiad (flagship, Dido-class light cruiser)
Perth (Sydney-class light cruiser), RAN
Calcutta (Carlisle-class AA cruiser)
Carlisle (Carlisle-class AA cruiser)
Juno (J/K/N-class destroyer)
Kingston (J/K/N-class destroyer)
Kandahar (J/K/N-class destroyer)
Nubian (Tribal-class destroyer)

EVENTS

1. 1130hrs: Force A1 (now incorporating Force B) patrols to the south-west of the Kythera Strait, and is under intermittent air attack throughout forenoon.

2. 1200hrs: Force C, having endured heavy air attacks all morning, heads at full speed towards the Kythera Strait.

3. 1225hrs: King requests Rawlings' battle fleet to come to his assistance. Consequently, Rawlings turns east and enters the Kythera Strait.

4. 1320hrs: Destroyer *Greyhound* is detached to intercept and destroy a caique spotted to the north.

5. 1332hrs: Force A1 comes under heavy air attack – *Warspite* is damaged.

6. 1335hrs: Forces A1 and C join up, and as the senior, King assumes command of the battle fleet.

7. 1351hrs: *Greyhound* is hit by a bomb and begins to sink. King sends destroyers *Kingston* and *Kandahar* to lend what assistance they can. He then sends Force B under Rowley to provide AA protection for the detached destroyers.

8. 1525hrs: The rescue force comes under heavy air attack: *Gloucester* is hit at 1527hrs, and loses her way. King orders *Fiji* and the two destroyers to leave her, and to rejoin the battle fleet. *Gloucester* will sink at 1715hrs.

9. 1600hrs: The battle fleet comes under heavy air attack for the remainder of the afternoon. Its speed is limited due to damaged vessels. The battleship *Valiant* is damaged. All ships are now running short of AA ammunition.

10. 1620hrs: *Fiji*, *Kingston* and *Kandahar* come under air attack as they steam south, having lost visual contact with battle fleet. Air attacks continue throughout the evening, until *Fiji* is sunk to the south of Crete at 2015hrs.

A representation by Lieutenant-Commander Rowland Langmaid of the last fight of HMS *Fiji*, namesake of her class. Having expended all of her AA ammunition earlier that day, *Fiji's* crew were reduced to firing flares and starshells at the enemy bombers, in a vain attempt to keep them at bay.

torpedoes to be jettisoned before the air attacks began in earnest. Another bomb hit wrecked the port 2-pdr pom-pom, and went on to explode below decks. By then, Rowley's cruiser had expended all its ammunition, and her remaining AA gunners were reduced to firing starshells at the approaching dive-bombers. Finally, just before 1545hrs, and watched by the ships of the nearby battle fleet, *Gloucester* was hit by three more bombs. These set off secondary explosions, which in turn fuelled the fires raging on her decks. It was now clear that the cruiser was doomed. So, Rowley gave the order to abandon ship.

As the stricken ship slowed to a halt, the ship's boats were lowered, but were too badly damaged to be of much use. *Fiji* steamed by, dropping Carley floats, while others were thrown from *Gloucester*, together with anything that could float. Captain William-Powlett of the *Fiji* realized he could do nothing more, and so he sped on towards the south, accompanied by *Kandahar* and *Kingston*. The *Gloucester* was left to die alone. By then, she was listing heavily to port, although she remained that way for some time, allowing more of her crew to scramble overboard. Even then, German bombers were still attacking the sinking cruiser, and the near misses set off shock waves that claimed the lives of many of the men in the water. At least one 250kg bomb struck the cruiser's bow, the aircraft coming so close that one survivor could make out the pilot's face.

Finally, at 1715hrs, the cruiser rolled over on her port side, and the last of her surviving crew threw themselves into the water. Among the last to leave his ship was Captain Rowley. Minutes later, *Gloucester* capsized, and then slowly went down by the stern. One of the survivors recalled that the water felt agreeably warm. A few aircraft strafed the rafts, but generally the survivors were left alone. As the hours passed, though, their numbers decreased as fatigue took its toll. By daybreak on Friday morning, only a handful were left. In all, 85 of her 815-strong crew survived the sinking, either by reaching one of the islands in the Kythera Strait, or by being picked up by a caique commandeered by the Germans. Captain Rowley's body washed up on the Egyptian coast three weeks later.

At 1715hrs on the evening of 22 May, HMS *Gloucester* rolled over onto her port side, turned turtle and then sank by the stern. This blurred, hastily snapped picture taken from the deck of the *Fiji* as she sped away to the south is the last image taken of the cruiser before she sank.

Meanwhile, King's battle fleet had been subjected to a succession of attacks that afternoon, which only drew to a close at 1510hrs, just 17 minutes before *Gloucester* was first hit. There was a brief lull, but as *Fiji*, *Kandahar* and *Kingston* continued to race towards the fleet, the German planes returned. From 1620hrs on, the fleet was subjected to a series of high-level attacks from LG 2 and KG 2. Most of these bombs missed their targets, but at 1645hrs the battleship *Valiant* was hit twice, with both bombs landing on her after superstructure and quarterdeck. The damage was not serious enough to impair the ship's ability to fight, and the fires caused by the explosions were soon put out. By 1712hrs, *Valiant*'s commanding officer Captain Charles Morgan was able to signal Rawlings that everything was under control. It might have been on board *Valiant*, but generally, as that afternoon wore on, the overall situation facing the British was still a desperate one.

Only the arrival of night would bring an end to the relentless air attacks. Dusk was at 2020hrs that evening, with full darkness coming just over an hour later at 2123hrs. That, though, was another 4¼ hours away. Until then, the battered warships had to survive as best they could. So, by 1800hrs, as the afternoon watch on the ships gave way to the dog watches, the various British naval groups continued their withdrawal to the south: King's Force C, with the rear admiral in overall control of the whole battle fleet, and Force A1 which accompanied it but remained under the control of Rawlings. Some 30 miles away to the east was Captain William-Powlett's *Fiji*, accompanied by the destroyers *Kandahar* and *Kashmir*. Almost all of these ships had virtually no AA ammunition left. Shortly after 1600hrs, as the air attacks were at their height, the battle fleet had been reinforced by another small naval force, Captain Lord Louis Mountbatten's 15th Destroyer Flotilla, whose flagship *Kelly* was accompanied by *Jackal*, *Kashmir*, *Kelvin* and *Kipling*. Mountbatten's ships were incorporated into Force C, greatly strengthening the defensive capabilities of King's battle fleet.

At 1710hrs, William-Powlett sent a radio message to King, reporting *Fiji*'s position as 24 miles west-north-west of Cape Elaphonisi, the south-western tip of Crete. He added that *Kandahar* and *Kashmir* were still accompanying the cruiser, and that his heading was 175°, and he was making 24 knots.

Operations to the west of Crete, 22–23 May 1941

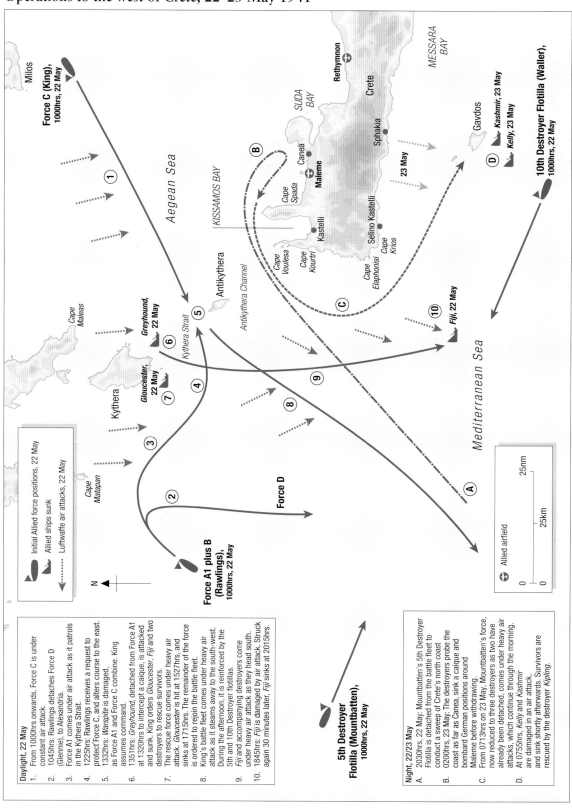

Force C (King),
1000hrs, 22 May

Milos

Aegean Sea

Rethymnon

Crete

MESSARA BAY

SUDA BAY

Canea
Maleme

Sphakia

Selino Kastelli

Gavdos

10th Destroyer Flotilla (Waller),
1000hrs, 22 May

Kashmir, 23 May
Kelly, 23 May

KISSAMOS BAY

Cape Spada

Kastelli

Cape Voulesa
Cape Kourtri

Cape Elaphonisi
Cape Krios

23 May

Antikythera

Cape Maleas

Greyhound,
22 May

Gloucester,
22 May

Kythera

Kythera Strait

Antikythera Channel

Fiji, 22 May

Mediterranean Sea

Cape Matapan

Force D

Force A1 plus B
(Rawlings),
1000hrs, 22 May

- Initial Allied force positions, 22 May
- Allied ships sunk
- Luftwaffe air attacks, 22 May

N

5th Destroyer
Flotilla (Mountbatten),
1000hrs, 22 May

Allied airfield

0   25nm
0   25km

Daylight, 22 May
1. From 1000hrs onwards, Force C is under constant air attack.
2. 1045hrs: Rawlings detaches Force D (Glennie), to Alexandria.
3. Force A1 comes under air attack as it patrols in the Kythera Strait.
4. 1225hrs: Rawlings receives a request to protect Force C, and alters course to the east.
5. 1332hrs: *Warspite* is damaged, as Force A1 and Force C combine. King assumes command.
6. 1351hrs: *Greyhound,* detached from Force A1 at 1320hrs to intercept a caique, is attacked and sunk. King orders *Gloucester, Fiji* and two destroyers to rescue survivors.
7. The rescue force comes under heavy air attack. *Gloucester* is hit at 1527hrs, and sinks at 1715hrs. The remainder of the force is ordered to rejoin the battle fleet.
8. King's battle fleet comes under heavy air attack as it steams away to the south-west. During the afternoon, it is reinforced by the 5th and 10th Destroyer flotillas.
9. *Fiji* and accompanying destroyers come under heavy air attack as they head south.
10. 1845hrs: *Fiji* is damaged by air attack. Struck again 30 minutes later, *Fiji* sinks at 2015hrs.

Night, 22/23 May
A. 2030hrs, 22 May: Mountbatten's 5th Destroyer Flotilla is detached from the battle fleet to conduct a sweep of Crete's north coast
B. 0200hrs, 23 May: The destroyers probe the coast as far as Canea, sink a caique and bombard German positions around Maleme before withdrawing.
C. From 0713hrs on 23 May, Mountbatten's force, now reduced to three destroyers as two have already been detached, comes under heavy air attacks, which continue through the morning.
D. At 0755hrs, *Kelly* and *Kashmir* are damaged in an air attack, and sink shortly afterwards. Survivors are rescued by the destroyer *Kipling.*

That placed him roughly 30 miles due east of the battle fleet, which was on a south-westerly course of 215°. That meant the two groups of ships were actually drawing further apart. It was 2100hrs before King remedied this, and altered course towards the east-south-east just as darkness was falling. By that time, though, it was too late to help the *Fiji*. Throughout that afternoon and early evening, the Luftwaffe attacks had continued, although by this time they had further to fly – by 1900hrs, when William-Powlett sent his signal, his cruiser was almost 100 miles due south of the German airfield at Molaoi.

This did not mean the attacks ceased, or even weakened. Later, it was reckoned that the cruiser had been subjected to at least two air attacks since leaving the sinking *Gloucester*. She was now completely out of AA ammunition, and her gun crews were reduced to firing starshells and flares at the enemy aircraft. William-Powlett was well aware that his only defence now was speed and manoeuvrability. Up to that moment, though, her luck had held. At 1730hrs, he turned towards the south-east, heading directly towards Alexandria. For the next hour or so, until 1845hrs, she was only subjected to two high-level attacks by flight-sized groups of bombers. Thanks to good ship-handling, though, the cruiser avoided the falling sticks of bombs. Then, at 1845hrs, *Fiji*'s luck ran out. An Me 109 from II./JG 77 had been looking for her for some time, and was running low on fuel. Her pilot was about to turn back to Molaoi when he spotted the cruiser and two destroyers through a gap in the low clouds.

He was carrying a 250kg bomb, and so he began a shallow dive towards the cruiser. His bombing run was judged to perfection – thanks to the cloud, *Fiji*'s crew did not spot the fighter until it was too late. The Messerschmitt released its bomb, then banked sharply away. William-Powlett was turning his ship hard to port, and the bomb missed, but exploded off the port side amidships. The blast blew in some of the plates in *Fiji*'s lower hull, which caused extensive flooding, and made the cruiser list heavily to port. One of the flooded compartments was a boiler room, which had to be shut down, reducing the cruiser's speed to just 17 knots. This made it much harder to avoid any further attacks. Still, William-Powlett nursed his ship on towards the safety of the south-west, and the coming of night.

However, at 1915hrs, another aircraft appeared, a second bomb-armed Me 109. The fighter swooped in fast, and once again William-Powlett had little chance to react. His single 250kg bomb penetrated one of the cruiser's boiler rooms and exploded. *Fiji* was already listing, but she now leaned further over, and fires blazed up amidships. Then the bomber returned to strafe the stricken ship with her 20mm cannons. The order was given to abandon ship. One of the survivors, Leading Seaman Clem Walker, recalled: 'The ship continued to list, and sailors were throwing overboard anything that would float, and jumping into the sea.' He added that at that point another aircraft approached and dropped two more bombs. This was most probably a Ju 88 from LG 2, which more likely dropped four 250kg bombs, and two of them hit the ship. Walker saw the two bombs strike the ship near 'Y' turret, and remembered they were black with white noses, with a red ring around them. The time was now approximately 2005hrs – shortly before dusk.

At 2015hrs, *Fiji* rolled over onto her port side, and lay in the water for a minute or so before rolling over and sinking. Dusk was now falling, but the risk of further air attacks remained. So, *Kandahar* and *Kingston* drew as

Captain Lord Louis Mountbatten, a distant member of the British royal family, proved an able flotilla commander during the Crete campaign, but lost two of his destroyers (*Kelly* and *Kashmir*) while returning from a night-time sweep of the north of the island. He and his men were rescued by another of his destroyers, the *Kipling*.

close as they could to the men in the water, and dropped Carley floats over the side, together with all of their boats. They then sped away to the south, to await nightfall. Commander William Robson of *Kandahar*, the senior of the two captains, returned shortly before 2100hrs, and the destroyer crews began picking up survivors. One of the men who helped was Commander Marshall-A'Deane, the commanding officer of *Greyhound* who was on board *Kandahar*, and seeing a wounded man struggling to climb a rope over the destroyer's side, he dived in to help. He never resurfaced. In the end, the two destroyers rescued 523 of *Fiji*'s complement of 780 officers and men. Captain William-Powlett was among those pulled from the water, and lived to tell the tale.

At 2245hrs, Robson's two destroyers left the area where *Fiji* had sunk, and headed south to join Rear Admiral King's battle fleet, which was 50 miles away. The coming of darkness brought an end to the day's misery for the Mediterranean Fleet. Since dawn, it had lost two cruisers and a destroyer, while two battleships and four cruisers had been damaged, along with several destroyers. While this battle had been raging at sea, the fighting had also been severe on land. On Crete, the Germans had managed to fly in reinforcements, and were now driving the defenders back. In Alexandria, Cunningham and his staff tried to take stock of the day's events, and to plan for a resumption of the naval battle the following day. What was clear, though, was that until the battle fleet had rearmed and refueled, it was in no condition to resume its battle with VIII.Fliegerkorps.

MOUNTBATTEN'S SORTIE

At 2030hrs that evening, just after sunset, Rear Admiral King detached Mountbatten and his five destroyers to head north and search for survivors from the three lost ships. *Kelly*, *Kashmir* and *Kipling* headed to the spot where *Fiji* had sunk, while *Kelvin* and *Jackal* steered for the Kythera Strait. However, after a radio report from Commander Robson in *Kashmir*, King cancelled his order, and instead instructed Mountbatten to pass through the Kythera Strait with his whole force and sweep the northern coast of Crete as far as Canea. *Kipling* developed a steering problem and was ordered south again, while the other four destroyers pressed on. When they reached Canea, *Kelly* and *Kashmir* destroyed two caiques and bombarded Maleme airfield, while *Kelvin* and *Jackal* found nothing in Kissamos Bay to the west, and returned to the open sea. They eventually returned safely to Alexandria.

A little after 2200hrs, King ordered Rawlings to detach two more destroyers, *Defender* and *Jaguar*, who were carrying stores and ammunition for the Royal Marines in Suda Bay. They would linger in the Ionian Sea until evening, and then make a fast passage through the Kythera Strait to Suda, hand their cargo to the garrison at Suda, and then speed back out to sea before dawn. Another relief attempt, a night-time landing at Tymbaki

on the southern coast of Crete, had been delayed as the naval situation deteriorated. At dawn, though, the Landing Ship *Glenroy*, laden with 900 troops accompanied by the AA cruiser *Coventry* and two small sloops, was still at sea well to the south of Crete. Later that day, the operation would be cancelled, and the expedition returned to Alexandria. Finally, when Mountbatten's original orders were cancelled, King ordered another group of reinforcements – Captain Waller's 10th Destroyer Flotilla – to search for survivors from *Fiji*. So, the three Australian destroyers *Stuart*, *Voyager* and *Vendetta* were sent north to take the place of *Kandahar* and *Kingston*.

King had expected to linger to the south of Crete, to provide a rallying point for Mountbatten's flotilla when it returned. Instead, though, at 0500hrs, the battle fleet was ordered back to Alexandria. Thanks to a badly worded

The leader of Captain Lord Mountbatten's 5th Destroyer Flotilla was the J/K/N-class destroyer HMS *Kelly*. She led the flotilla's four other destroyers on a patrol off Crete's north coast, but at daybreak was still off the south-west corner of Crete, and therefore well within range of VIII.Fliegerkorps.

Under Commander Hilary Biggs, the G/H/I-class destroyer HMS *Hero* took part in the Greece evacuation, and formed part of Force A1 during the campaign. *Hero* was then detached to spirit the Greek king and his family to safety, who had been on Crete when the German invasion began.

THE SINKING OF HMS *KELLY*, 23 MAY 1941 (PP. 70–71)

Late on 'Black Thursday' (22 May), as the British battle fleet withdrew, Rear Admiral King detached Captain Lord Louis Mountbatten's 5th Destroyer Flotilla to conduct a night-time sweep to the north of Crete. This was successful, but his five destroyers became divided, and so by dawn, as Mountbatten headed south down the western coast of Crete, his own destroyer *Kelly* was only accompanied by her sister ships *Kashmir* and *Kipling*. Soon afterwards, the destroyers were spotted by the Luftwaffe. Mountbatten's ships evaded several attacks by high-flying Ju 88 bombers, but at 0755hrs two squadrons of Ju 87 'Stukas' from I./StG 2 appeared, and began their attack. The destroyers' fast evasive manoeuvres saved them from being hit by the first two waves, but their luck ran out during the third attack.

Kashmir (**1**) was hit amidships, and she immediately began to founder. Minutes later, *Kelly* (**2**) was struck too, a 250kg bomb exploding aft beside 'X' turret. Her engines were still running as she capsized. Shown here is the scene moments after *Kelly* was hit. She is already listing heavily to port, while a fourth wave of 'Stukas' (**3**) begin their own attack. On *Kelly*'s bridge, Mountbatten gives the order to abandon ship.

signal, Mountbatten thought the whole battle fleet was out of ammunition, hence his order to retire. In fact, Force A1 could have remained on station and protected the destroyers. Instead, Mountbatten's flotilla was left to its own devices. He ordered *Kelly* and *Kashmir* to pass through the Kythera Strait, and continue south past Cape Elaphonisi.

That night, the fleet had also been active to the east of Crete. Captain Mack's Force E (the destroyers *Havock*, *Ilex*, *Jervis* and the Australian *Nizam*) had slipped through the Kasos Strait and had probed the northern coast of Crete again, as far as Heraklion. They were spotted off the north-east coast of Crete at dawn, and were subjected to five hours of bombing by German and Italian aircraft operating from Rhodes and Scarpanto. Although none of the destroyers were hit, both *Havock* and *Ilex* had been damaged by near misses. Two other naval operations had taken place that night. At 2030hrs, Cunningham had ordered Rawlings to detach *Decoy* and *Hero* from Force A1 and send them to the fishing village of Agia Roumeli on the southern coast of Crete. There the destroyers embarked King George II of Greece and his family, along with other British and Greek officials, and then rejoined the battle fleet.

As dawn broke on Friday 23 May, Mountbatten was through the strait and heading south with his two destroyers down the north-western coast of Crete. A third destroyer, *Kipling*, had just rejoined them. His two other destroyers *Kelvin* and *Jackal* were already to the south of Crete, heading towards Alexandria. Far to the south, the battle fleet had become separated, with Force A1 to the west of Force C. King planned to join forces with Rawlings, and then the combined force would set a course for Alexandria. In the meantime, Rawlings hoped to offer whatever support he could to his detached destroyers. Two of these, *Kandahar* and *Kingston*, were already within sight of Force C. Waller's three destroyers were a little further to the north, while *Defender* and *Jaguar* were now approaching Suda Bay. This meant that despite Cunningham's order to regroup and return to Alexandria, the fleet was still widely scattered. This suited the Luftwaffe perfectly.

Mountbatten's three destroyers were spotted soon after dawn, and the air attacks began at 0713hrs. The first two attacks were high-level ones, each from a squadron-sized formation of Ju 88s from LG 1, flying at around 2,500m. The second one came about 15 minutes after the first, but on both occasions the destroyers, manoeuvering at high speed, managed to avoid the bombs. The destroyers had been racing southwards all this time, and by 0755hrs were south of Cape Elaphonisi, and to the east of the small island of Gavdos. It was then that the Ju 87s appeared – two squadrons of them, from I./StG 2. Leading the attack was Staffelkapitän Hubertus Hitschhold, who split his dive-bombers into eight flights. Two of these would attack the destroyers from different directions at the same time. The three destroyers managed to evade the first waves, but on the third run *Kashmir* was hit amidships.

A Ju 87 Stuka dive-bomber releasing its bomb. The Stuka's drawback was its poor field of vision while carrying out its dive. Enterprising warship commanders found it possible to manoeuvre their ships to pass underneath the dive-bomber, and so throw off its aim.

The 250kg bomb broke the destroyer's back, and she sank quickly. Commander King gave the order to abandon ship, but one gunner stayed at his post, and shot down a Stuka with his 20mm Oerlikon gun. This enraged the German airmen, who began buzzing the wreck, and machine-gunned the men in the water. *Kelly* was hit by the fourth wave, when a bomb landed on top of one of her after mounts. Mountbatten's flagship began heeling over, while her engines were still racing, and then she capsized. She remained there for some time before sinking, but again the Germans strafed the survivors in the water. During a lull, Commander Aubrey St Clair-Ford in *Kipling* brought his destroyer in to pick up survivors. He broke off as a final attack was launched, but returned once the Germans flew off. Over the next hour, he rescued 282 men from the two destroyers, including both Mountbatten and King. At 1100hrs, after all survivors were on board, *Kipling* headed back to Alexandria, although she continued to be attacked as Crete faded from view astern.

Low cloud over the Ionian Sea also allowed *Defender* and *Jaguar* to avoid detection. To the south, Rawlings' and King's forces had been reunited, and the battle fleet was now on its way to Alexandria. *Kandahar* and *Kingston*, carrying survivors from *Greyhound* and *Fiji*, rejoined the fleet soon after dawn. They were desperately low on fuel, but were able to replenish from the battleships. At 0800hrs, *Decoy* and *Hero* also rejoined the fleet, with the Greek royal family embarked. Waller's three Australian destroyers joined them later that morning. King learned of the sinking of *Kelly* and *Kashmir* from St Clair-Ford on *Kipling*, but was assured all had been done to save their crews. So, the fleet maintained its course for Alexandria.

For Cunningham, it had been another bruising day. He had lost two more destroyers, and his battle fleet, although heading back to port, was effectively out of action until it could be refueled and resupplied. News from Crete itself was also bad – Suda Bay had been attacked that Friday, and the five boats of the 10th Motor Torpedo Boat Flotilla had been destroyed, along with

During the Crete campaign the newly commissioned fast minelayer HMS *Abdiel* proved to be one of the most versatile warships in the fleet. *Abdiel* was used to transport stores and men to Crete, and then to evacuate the soldiers, as well as functioning in her intended role. As Captain the Hon. Edward Pleydell-Bouverie's minelayer could make 40 knots, *Abdiel* was ideally suited for these fast night-time missions.

the armed trawler *Syvern*. It was clear that the fleet could no longer prevent German reinforcements from reaching the island by sea without risking even greater losses. It would be hard-pressed to supply or reinforce the Allied troops on the island. Still, Cunningham was a determined man. His signal to the fleet on the evening of 'Black Thursday' read: 'Stick it out. Navy must not let army down. No enemy forces must reach Crete by sea.' Now, a day later, Cunningham was still adamant that his fleet would do its duty, come what may. It is fortunate, then, that the fleet was spared even greater losses thanks to the rapidly deteriorating military situation on Crete.

The Illustrious-class fleet aircraft carrier HMS *Formidable* lacked the embarked aircraft she needed to properly support the Mediterranean Fleet's operations around Crete. *Formidable* was also unable to protect herself when attacked to the south of Crete on 26 May.

KEEPING UP THE PRESSURE

During the night, *Defender* and *Jaguar* had made their fast passage through the Kythera Strait to Suda Bay, unloaded their stores there, and then left again by way of the Kasos Strait. On their leg from Suda to Alexandria, they carried 250 naval base staff. By mid-morning of Saturday 24 May, they were out of danger. The fleet had also reached Alexandria safely, although *Kipling* had run out of fuel 50 miles out and had to be towed in. As the business of replenishing the ships began, their exhausted crews grabbed what sleep they could. For Cunningham, though, there would be no time for such luxuries. That morning he had sent the cruisers *Ajax* and *Dido* back to sea, accompanied by the destroyers *Imperial*, *Kimberley* and *Hotspur*. While he had already informed the Admiralty that due to enemy air superiority the fleet was unable to operate in Cretan waters in daylight, he was determined to prevent the enemy reinforcing the island by sea. So, Captain Desmond McCarthy of *Ajax*, commanding the force, was to conduct another night sweep along Crete's northern coast.

Similarly, the fast minelayer *Abdiel* was sent to Suda to land reinforcements and stores there during the night of 24/25 May. Meanwhile, a handful of

In May 1941, the main fighter available to the Fleet Air Arm was the Fairey Fulmar. A squadron of Fulmars was embarked in the fleet carrier *Formidable*, but the two on Combat Air Patrol over the carrier on 26 May were unable to protect her when she was attacked to the south of Crete.

aircraft had been embarked on the carrier *Formidable*, which meant he could provide his ships with limited air cover. She duly became the flagship of Vice Admiral Pridham-Wippell's Force A, and put to sea on Sunday morning, accompanied by the battleships *Barham* and *Queen Elizabeth* and eight destroyers. Cunningham's intention was that *Formidable* would launch an air strike on the airfield on Scarpanto and then retire to the south, where it would await further orders.

The news that weekend, though, was unremittingly grim. For the Navy the biggest blow was the loss of the battlecruiser *Hood*, sunk early on Saturday morning by the German battleship *Bismarck*. However, the military situation on Crete was also deteriorating rapidly. It became clear that the army was being hard-pressed. So, on Sunday evening the landing ship *Glenroy* sailed from Alexandria with 800 reinforcements for the Cretan garrison on board. Force A would cover its passage to Crete, once the Scarpanto raid was completed. That night, McCarthy's destroyers and cruisers slipped through the Kasos Strait unobserved, and entered the Aegean Sea. Their night sweep as far as Suda was uneventful, as was their passage back through the strait. By dawn on Sunday, McCarthy's force was safely out of sight of the island.

Cunningham ordered McCarthy to remain to the south-east of Crete throughout the day, and to repeat the sweep the following night, 25/26 May. So, as Force A sailed towards Scarpanto, and *Abdiel* unloaded her men and stores, McCarthy repeated his night-time sweep. Once again, though, no enemy convoy was sighted. By dawn on Monday 26 May, as McCarthy's cruisers and destroyers were heading southwards through the Kasos Strait, Force A reached its launch point 100 miles south-south-west of Scarpanto. Only nine planes were available, though, and while these destroyed two Italian bombers on the ground and damaged several others, the overall effect of the raid was negligible except in terms of boosting British morale. Once the aircraft had been recovered, and once McCarthy's force had rendezvoused with him, Pridham-Wippell ordered Force A to head south, to await further orders. McCarthy's destroyers, though, were sent back to Alexandria to refuel.

This move to the south might have put Pridham-Wippell's ships out of range of VIII.Fliegerkorps, but it brought Force A closer to the coast of North Africa. At 1320hrs, *Formidable*'s radar picked up multiple aircraft contacts approaching from the south. These were 17 Ju 87s from II./StG 2 and 11 Ju 88s from III./LG 1. The day before, Richthofen had sent them to North Africa so they could use X.Fliegerkorps' bases there to attack the British south of Crete. The carrier's four serviceable Fulmar fighters were flown off, and these managed to shoot down three Stukas for the loss of one fighter. This, though, was not enough to stop the remaining 17 dive-bombers from reaching the carrier. Most of the bombs missed, but two struck *Formidable* on her starboard side, with one 1,000kg bomb landing on the forward flight deck, and a second striking the gun battery mounted on her starboard quarter before exploding outboard of the ship. A major fire forward was eventually extinguished, and flooding dealt with. The carrier was badly damaged, and while flying operations continued, it was clear that *Formidable* had effectively been put out of action. She would remain so until the end of the year.

Another casualty of the attack was the destroyer *Nubian*. She was hit by a 250kg bomb dropped by a Ju 88, which exploded on the destroyer's stern. Her rudder was destroyed, but her propeller shafts still turned. So, after Commander Ravenhill and his crew fought to keep their ship afloat, he used his engines to steer the crippled destroyer, which was eventually escorted into Alexandria. It would be November 1942 before she returned to service. On the following day, Tuesday 27 May, Force A came under heavy air attack again, this time from 15 Ju 88s and He 111s of LG 1 operating from Scarpanto and Rhodes. They struck shortly before 0900hrs. A 250kg bomb from a Ju 88 struck *Barham* on the roof of 'Y' turret, causing a major fire which claimed one life and took two hours to extinguish. Several near misses also buckled her anti-torpedo bulges, which had to be flooded to prevent the battleship from listing. She, too, would be out of action until the end of the year. As a result, at 1230hrs, Cunningham recalled Force A to Alexandria. It returned to port at 2100hrs that evening.

THE EVACUATION

Meanwhile, the situation on Crete had deteriorated. Since Saturday, thanks to the arrival of reinforcements, the Germans had increased the pressure on the Allied defenders to the west of Canea, and by Monday morning their defences were breached. They withdrew to a new defensive line closer to Canea and Suda, but it was clear that this would not hold much longer. The reinforcements landed from *Abdiel* on 26/27 May were too few to turn the tide. The defences began to break that evening. On the morning of Monday 26 May, in a meeting on board *Warspite*, both General Wavell and Air Chief Marshall Tedder advocated ordering the surrender of the Crete garrison. The cost to the Navy of evacuating the troops would be too high. Only Cunningham disagreed. According to Commander Thomas Brownrigg of the admiral's staff, Cunningham declared:

> It has always been the duty of the Navy to take the army overseas to battle, and if the army fail, to bring them back again. If we now break with that tradition, ever afterwards when soldiers go overseas they will tend to look over their shoulders instead of relying on the Navy. You have said, General [Wavell], that it will take three years to build a new fleet. I will tell you that it

The evacuation, 23 May–1 June 1941

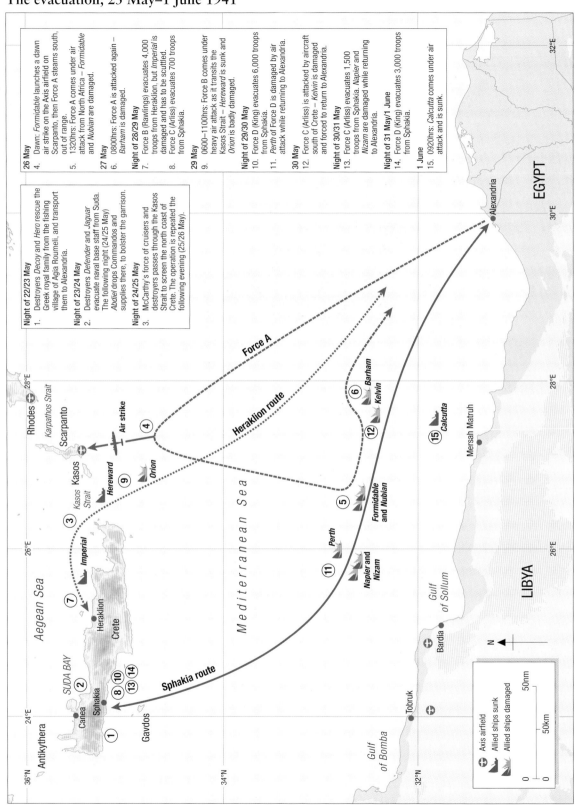

Night of 22/23 May
1. Destroyers *Decoy* and *Hero* rescue the Greek royal family from the fishing village of Agia Roumeli, and transport them to Alexandria.

Night of 23/24 May
2. Destroyers *Defender* and *Jaguar* evacuate naval base staff from Suda. The following night (24/25 May) *Abdiel* drops Commandos and supplies there, to bolster the garrison.

Night of 24/25 May
3. McCarthy's force of cruisers and destroyers passes through the Kasos Strait to screen the north coast of Crete. The operation is repeated the following evening (25/26 May).

26 May
4. Dawn: *Formidable* launches a dawn air strike on the Axis airfield on Scarpanto, then Force A steams south, out of range.
5. 1320hrs: Force A comes under air attack from North Africa – *Formidable* and *Nubian* are damaged.

27 May
6. 0800hrs: Force A is attacked again – *Barham* is damaged.

Night of 28/29 May
7. Force B (Rawlings) evacuates 4,000 troops from Heraklion, but *Imperial* is damaged and has to be scuttled.
8. Force C (Arliss) evacuates 700 troops from Sphakia.

29 May
9. 0600–1100hrs: Force B comes under heavy air attack as it transits the Kasos Strait – *Hereward* is sunk and *Orion* is badly damaged.

Night of 29/30 May
10. Force D (King) evacuates 6,000 troops from Sphakia.
11. *Perth* of Force D is damaged by air attack while returning to Alexandria.

30 May
12. Force C (Arliss) is attacked by aircraft south of Crete – *Kelvin* is damaged and forced to return to Alexandria.

Night of 30/31 May
13. Force C (Arliss) evacuates 1,500 troops from Sphakia. *Napier* and *Nizam* are damaged while returning to Alexandria.

Night of 31 May/1 June
14. Force D (King) evacuates 3,000 troops from Sphakia.

1 June
15. 0920hrs: *Calcutta* comes under air attack and is sunk.

will take three hundred years to build a new tradition. If, gentlemen, you now order the army in Crete to surrender, the fleet will still go there to bring off the Marines.

As Cunningham himself said later: 'My view was perfectly clear.' That was the end of the argument. At 0824hrs the following morning, Wavell informed the Prime Minister that the position on Crete was no longer tenable, and that the island had to be evacuated. Despite Churchill's obstinacy, his chiefs of staff approved the decision. So, it was now the job of Cunningham and his fleet to return to Crete, and to rescue the Crete garrison, regardless of the cost. There were, though, limits to what Cunningham was prepared to risk. The air superiority of the Luftwaffe meant that the evacuation would have to be carried out at night. Also, if the bulk of the evacuees could reach the south coast of Crete, it would avoid the much more dangerous passage through the Kasos Strait. In the end, though, largely thanks to the recent experience of Greece, this evacuation proved a relatively straightforward enterprise, albeit a costly one.

At 0600hrs on Wednesday 28 May, Rawlings, commanding Force B, left Alexandria for Heraklion. His flagship *Orion* was accompanied by *Ajax* and *Dido* and six destroyers (*Decoy*, *Jackal*, *Imperial*, *Hotspur*, *Hereward* and *Kimberley*). At 0800hrs, Force C, under Captain Stephen Arliss of the destroyer *Napier*, left for Sphakia on Crete's south coast, accompanied by *Nizam*, *Kandahar* and *Kelvin*. Arliss arrived off Sphakia at 0030hrs on Thursday, and after landing food and supplies for the army, he embarked 700 men. He returned to sea at 0300hrs, but despite being attacked by four Ju 88s from LG 1 at 0900hrs, Force C reached Alexandria safely at 1700hrs that evening. *Napier* suffered minor damage during the attack.

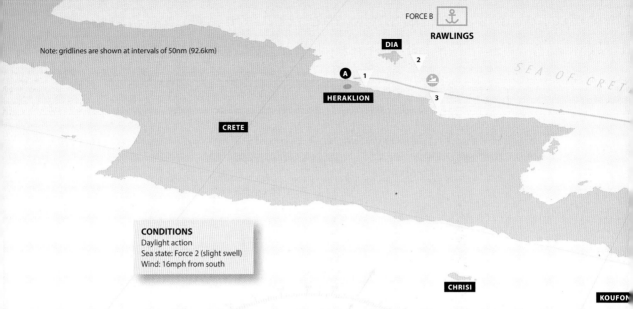

Note: gridlines are shown at intervals of 50nm (92.6km)

FORCE B ⚓

RAWLINGS

SEA OF CRETE

DIA

2

A 1

HERAKLION

3

CRETE

CONDITIONS
Daylight action
Sea state: Force 2 (slight swell)
Wind: 16mph from south

CHRISI

KOUFON

EVENTS

1. 0320hrs: Force B leaves Heraklion, with 4,000 troops embarked on its nine warships.

2. 0342hrs: Destroyer *Imperial* develops steering problems. Destroyer *Hotspur* is detached to support her, while the remainder of Force B continues on towards the Kasos Strait.

3. 0445hrs: After damage to *Imperial* is deemed irreparable, her crew and soldiers are transferred to *Hotspur*, and the crippled destroyer is sunk by two torpedoes. *Hotspur* then speeds after the rest of Force B.

4. 0600hrs: *Hotspur* rejoins Force B, which has been making 15 knots to allow her to catch up. Simultaneously, *Dido*'s radar detects aircraft approaching from the north-east. Rawlings orders Force B to increase speed to 30 knots.

5. 0605hrs: First air attack of the morning: a squadron of 12 Stukas from StG 2 based in Scarpanto attacks the British ships. Destroyer *Decoy* is damaged by a near miss, and her speed is reduced to 25 knots. Rawlings orders a corresponding reduction in Force B's speed.

6. 0624hrs: Second attack, by two squadrons of StG 2 Stukas. *Hereward* is hit amidships, and forced to pull out of formation. Lieutenant-Commander Munn decides to attempt to beach his ship on the Cretan coast.

7. 0652hrs: Another attack by six Stukas targets *Hereward*, which is crippled by another hit. Munn orders his crew and passengers to abandon ship.

8. 0701hrs: Small groups of Stukas attack Force B, without scoring any hits.

9. 0710hrs: A squadron of Ju 88s from LG 1 based on Rhodes conducts a level bombing attack, but fails to hit any of the ships.

10. 0730hrs: A second larger Ju 88 attack is carried out, and *Orion* is damaged by a near miss. Consequently, the speed of Force B is reduced to 21 knots.

11. 0731hrs: During an attack by several Stukas, *Orion*'s bridge is strafed, and Captain Back is killed. Rear Admiral Rawlings is also lightly wounded, but continues to command the force.

12. 0745hrs: In another major attack by Stukas, *Orion* is hit again, and 'A' turret is knocked out. Moments later, *Dido* is also hit in the same area, and 'B' turret is put out of action.

13. 0755hrs: Following another dive-bomber attack on the cruisers, the enemy bombers return to their bases to rearm and refuel, giving the crews of Force B time to deal with any damage to their ships.

14. 1045hrs: A final Stuka attack by all of III./StG 2 scores only one hit, but a bomb strikes *Orion*'s bridge; the bomb explodes two decks below, where hundreds of evacuated soldiers are being quartered. Over 500 men are killed or wounded.

15. Force B undergoes three more long-range attacks from Ju 88s based on Rhodes as it heads back to Alexandria, but no more hits are achieved. The last attack is at 1500hrs.

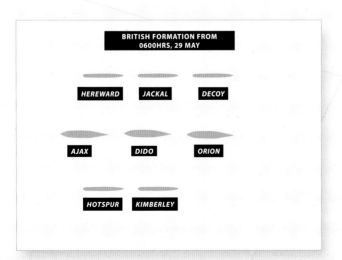

BRITISH FORMATION FROM 0600HRS, 29 MAY

HEREWARD   JACKAL   DECOY

AJAX   DIDO   ORION

HOTSPUR   KIMBERLEY

ROYAL NAVY
MEDITERRANEAN FLEET (ADMIRAL CUNNINGHAM, BASED IN ALEXANDRIA)
A. Force B (Rear Admiral Rawlings)
  Orion (flagship, Leander-class light cruiser)
  Ajax (Leander-class light cruiser)
  Dido (Dido-class AA cruiser)
  Decoy (D/E-class destroyer)
  Hereward (G/H/I-class destroyer)
  Hotspur (G/H/I-class destroyer)
  Imperial (G/H/I-class destroyer)
  Jackal (J/K/N-class destroyer)
  Kimberley (J/K/N-class destroyer)

FORCE B IN THE KASOS STRAIT, 29 MAY 1941

Late in the evening of 28 May, Rear Admiral Rawlings' Force B arrived off Heraklion, and began the business of evacuation. By 0320hrs the following morning they had embarked 4,000 troops, divided among the force's three cruisers and six destroyers. Dawn found Force B heading south through the Kasos Strait, dangerously close to Axis airfields on Rhodes and Scarpanto.

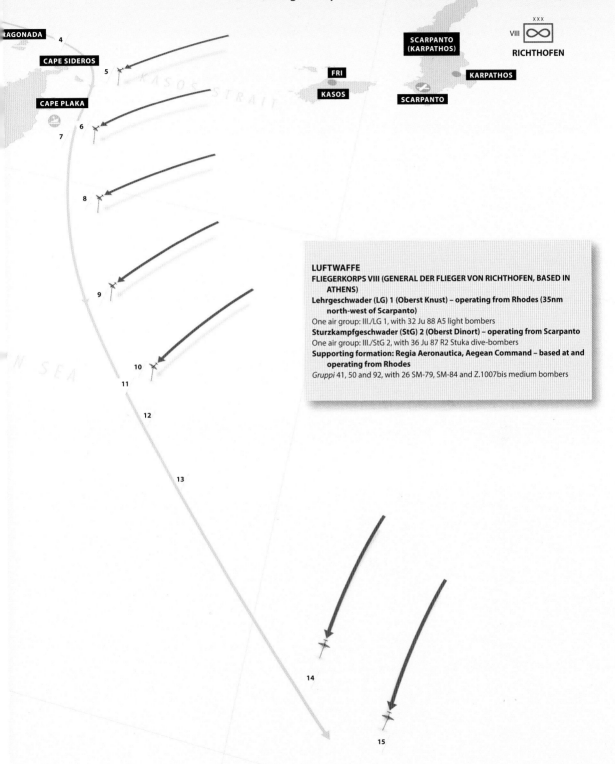

RAGONADA 4

CAPE SIDEROS 5

CAPE PLAKA 6

7

8

9

10

11

12

13

14

15

KASOS STRAIT

AEGEAN SEA

FRI

KASOS

SCARPANTO (KARPATHOS)

SCARPANTO

KARPATHOS

VIII ∞ RICHTHOFEN

XXX

LUFTWAFFE
FLIEGERKORPS VIII (GENERAL DER FLIEGER VON RICHTHOFEN, BASED IN ATHENS)
Lehrgeschwader (LG) 1 (Oberst Knust) – operating from Rhodes (35nm north-west of Scarpanto)
One air group: III./LG 1, with 32 Ju 88 A5 light bombers
Sturzkampfgeschwader (StG) 2 (Oberst Dinort) – operating from Scarpanto
One air group: III./StG 2, with 36 Ju 87 R2 Stuka dive-bombers
Supporting formation: Regia Aeronautica, Aegean Command – based at and operating from Rhodes
Gruppi 41, 50 and 92, with 26 SM-79, SM-84 and Z.1007bis medium bombers

The landing of evacuated Commonwealth troops from a destroyer in Alexandria. Although some were wounded, most had lost their equipment and all were exhausted, these troops survived to fight again, largely thanks to Cunningham's determination not to let down the army.

Rawlings, though, faced a tougher challenge. Force B was bombed on Wednesday evening as it passed through the Kasos Strait, and both *Ajax* and *Imperial* were damaged by near misses. However, this was not considered serious enough to warrant their return to Alexandria empty handed. Force B finally arrived off Heraklion at 2330hrs, and the business of ferrying the troops to the ships began. The embarkation took three hours, and it was not before 0320hrs on Thursday that Rawling's ships began their return voyage, laden with 4,000 troops. Just 25 minutes later, a signal from Lieutenant-Commander Charles de Winton Kitcat of *Imperial* reported a major steering malfunction – an undetected result of the bombing attack. Towing her to safety was unfeasible, and as the rest of the force steamed on, Lieutenant-Commander Cecil Brown in *Hotspur* was detached to deal with the situation. After the soldiers and crew were transferred, *Hotspur* finished off *Imperial* using two torpedoes. By this time, though, it was 0445hrs, and dawn was fast approaching.

Meanwhile, Force B made 15 knots to give *Hotspur* a chance to catch up. She overhauled Force B at 0600hrs, while they were heading south through the Kasos Strait, allowing Rawlings to order an increase of speed to 30 knots. Minutes later, the first German bombers appeared – StG 2's Stukas from Scarpanto. A near miss to *Decoy* caused flooding, which reduced the force's speed to 25 knots. About 20 minutes later, at 0625hrs a dive-bomber peeled off to attack the destroyer *Hereward*, on the port side of the formation. The Stuka's bomb hit the destroyer amidships, and she quickly lost power. Rawlings, though, was unwilling to risk the rest of his force to help her. *Hereward*'s captain, Lieutenant-Commander William Munn decided to

The G/H/I-class destroyer HMS *Hereward*, pictured shortly before the outbreak of war. She was used to evacuate Commonwealth troops from both Greece and Crete, but succumbed to air attack on 29 May, after being attacked in the Kasos Strait. As a result, the surviving crew and the destroyer's evacuated passengers were captured.

try to run her aground on the Cretan coast, 5 miles to the west. As the destroyer limped inshore, her plight drew the attention of another flight of dive-bombers. Munn and his crew fought back, but the ship was hit again, and sank. An hour later, the survivors, including 300 soldiers, were rescued by a patrol of Italian MAS boats.

More attacks from LG 1's Ju 88s followed, and at 0730hrs another near miss from a 250kg bomb damaged *Orion*, forcing another reduction to 21 knots. A minute later, a Stuka strafed *Orion*'s bridge, killing the cruiser's commanding officer Captain Geoffrey Back, and wounding Rawlings. At 0740hrs, another bomb landed next to the cruiser's forward turret, putting it out of action, while the same thing happened on *Dido*, thanks to a direct hit on 'B' turret, which killed one gunner and injured several more. At 0755hrs, the aircraft flew back to base to rearm; this gave the ships a respite, which they used to tend to the wounded, and deal with the fire and flooding on the two cruisers.

The Ju 87s returned with a vengeance at 1045hrs, just as Force B passed through the southern end of the strait. A whole squadron of them targeted *Orion*, and Commander Wynne, who was now in charge of the ship, managed to avoid all but one of them. It penetrated the open bridge to explode in a messdeck three decks below, which was crowded with soldiers. Some 260 men were killed in the blast and in the fires that followed, and another 280 wounded. Many of these suffered horrendous burns. Wynne was one of those killed, and so another officer took charge, supervising the damage-control teams and setting up an emergency bridge aft.

That was the last Stuka attack, but Force B had to endure three more attacks from Ju 88s before it drew out of range at 1500hrs. By then, though, two Fulmars had appeared, to give what air cover they could. A previous request from Rawlings to the RAF had been unproductive, although RAF Hurricanes patrolling over the Mediterranean had shot down two Ju 88s that afternoon. Rawlings' ships reached Alexandria at 2000hrs on Thursday evening, with his flagship still listing and reduced to 16 knots thanks to seawater getting into her ruptured fuel tanks. Of the 4,000 evacuees, almost 800 had been killed, wounded or captured during the voyage, two destroyers had been lost and two cruisers had been put out of action. The cost of the evacuation had been extremely high, but as Cunningham told Rawlings that evening, it had been worth it, to save the bulk of the Heraklion garrison.

The light cruiser *Orion* was commanded by Captain Geoffrey Back during the Crete campaign, and served as the flagship of Rear Admiral Rawlings during the evacuation of Crete. Back was killed along with hundreds of the cruiser's crew and embarked soldiers when her bridge superstructure was hit on 29 May.

FORCE B UNDER ATTACK IN THE KASOS STRAIT, 29 MAY 1941 (PP. 84–85)

On the night of 28/29 May, Rear Admiral Rawlings' Force B of three cruisers and six destroyers evacuated 4,000 troops from Heraklion, on Crete's north coast. The loss of a destroyer delayed them, and at dawn Force B was still in the Kasos Strait, to the east of Crete. As they steamed south towards safety, they were subjected to a succession of bombing attacks, which led to the sinking of another destroyer, and damage to several other ships. These included the cruisers *Orion* and *Dido*, both of which had a forward turret knocked out. The speed of the force dropped due to flooding damage to *Orion*, but Rawlings was determined to keep his remaining ships together for mutual protection. Then, at 1045hrs, as Force B passed through the southern end of the strait, it was attacked again, by Ju 87 'Stukas' from III./StG 2.

Shown here is the moment a 250kg bomb from one of these dive-bombers (**1**) strikes *Orion*'s bridge (**2**). In the explosion, over 500 soldiers and evacuated soldiers will be killed or wounded. Close astern of *Orion* is the already damaged AA cruiser *Dido* (**3**), while the destroyer *Jackal* (**4**) can be seen off her port beam.

On 29 May, the AA cruiser HMS *Dido*, the namesake of her class, was badly damaged in an air attack to the south-east of Crete. A 250kg bomb struck the roof of 'A' turret and wrecked it. However, Captain Henry McCall and his crew managed to deal with the resulting fires, and the ship continued providing AA cover for Rear Admiral Rawlings' force until it passed out of range of the enemy.

Meanwhile, the evacuation continued. At 2100hrs on Wednesday, Rear Admiral King sailed from Alexandria for Sphakia. His command, Force D, consisted of the cruisers *Phoebe*, *Perth* and *Calcutta*, the destroyers *Hasty*, *Janus* and *Jervis*, and the landing ship *Glengyle*. Their passage was uneventful, apart from an unsuccessful attack by a lone Ju 88, and Force D reached Sphakia at 2330hrs on Thursday 29 May. They left again at 0330hrs with 6,000 evacuees on board. At 0645hrs, King was reinforced by Captain Waller's destroyers *Defender*, *Jaguar* and *Stuart*. By that time, they were 100 miles away from the island. This time, the RAF showed up, and provided fighter cover for most of the day. They also shot down two He IIIs.

This support was welcome, as Force D was still in range of the Luftwaffe and was subjected to three air attacks between 0930hrs and 1112hrs. These assailants were a mixture of 12 Ju 88s and He 111s from LG 1, and eight Ju 87s from StG 2, based on Scarpanto. In the first of these attacks, the Australian cruiser *Perth* received a direct hit from a 250kg bomb, which penetrated her hull and put one of her boiler rooms out of action. Captain Philip Bowyer-Smith and his men managed to deal with the damage, though, and Force D eventually reached the safety of Alexandria that evening. That brought the total of men evacuated from Crete to a little under 10,000. Nevertheless, around 8,000 more men were still stranded around Sphakia. So, the evacuation would continue.

At 0930hrs on Friday 30 May, Captain Arliss' Force C slipped out of Alexandria for what would be the third nightly evacuation from Sphakia. His own Australian destroyer *Napier* was accompanied by another Australian one, the *Nizam*, as well as *Kandahar* and *Kelvin*. That morning, though, *Kandahar* developed engine problems and had to return to Alexandria. At 1530hrs, while 120 miles to the south of Crete, the three remaining destroyers were attacked by a flight of three Ju 88s, which approached unseen from astern. None of the bombs hit the ships, but *Kelvin* was damaged sufficiently by a near miss to warrant her return to port. The two remaining Australian destroyers arrived off Sphakia at 0030hrs on Saturday 31 May. They embarked 1,500 men, and the fully laden destroyers headed back out to sea

Under Lieutenant-Commander Max Clark RAN, the Australian J/K/N-class destroyer *Nizam* was part of Captain Mack's Force E, which bombarded Scarpanto (Karpathos) on 20–21 May, and then Captain Arliss' Force C, which evacuated troops from Sphakia one week later. *Nizam* was damaged by a near miss as she returned to Alexandria, laden with troops.

at 0300hrs. At 0815hrs, they were attacked by a flight of three Ju 88s, the first of four such attacks, which would last an hour. Both destroyers were damaged by near misses, but were spared a direct hit. Air cover protected them from 0900hrs on, and three German and one Italian bombers were shot down. Ten hours later, a weary Force C reached the safety of Alexandria.

Although 1,500 men had been saved, by the army's own estimates 6,500 more were still stranded on the beach at Sphakia. So, at 0600hrs on Saturday morning, as Arliss' destroyers headed home, Rear Admiral King's Force D put to sea again. This time he only had his flagship *Phoebe*, accompanied by *Abdiel*, *Hotspur*, *Jackal* and *Kimberley*. Before they sailed, the exhausted crews were given the chance to stay behind. None of them accepted. This time the RAF provided effective air cover during the outward voyage, and the voyage to Sphakia was uneventful. The ships anchored off the beach at 2320hrs on Saturday night, and began embarking as many men as they could take. By the time they raised anchor at 0300hrs on Sunday morning, over 3,000 men had been embarked. Once again, the RAF appeared at daybreak, and the fast passage home was as uneventful as the outward leg. Force C reached Alexandria at 1700hrs that evening.

However, there would be one last casualty of the campaign. At 0630hrs on Sunday 1 June, the AA cruisers *Calcutta* and *Coventry* left Alexandria to provide additional cover for King's ships. They were spotted by German reconnaissance planes operating from airfields in North Africa. At 0900hrs, when just 85 miles from the port, they spotted two Ju 88s on radar,

During the evacuation of the Crete garrison, the Dido-class AA cruiser *Phoebe*, commanded by Captain Guy Grantham, served as the flagship of Rear Admiral King's Force D. King successfully evacuated over 6,000 men from the beach at Sphakia during the night of 29/30 May.

approaching them from the north. They, too, had flown from North Africa, and were from III./LG 1. At 0920hrs, they approached the cruisers from the east, using the sun as cover. One of the bombers targeted *Coventry*, but its stick of four 250kg bombs missed her. *Calcutta* was less lucky – she was hit by two of the four bombs from the second bomber, which struck her amidships. *Calcutta* began settling fast, and so Captain Lees gave the order to abandon ship.

As the bombers flew off and *Coventry* lowered boats to pick up survivors, RAF Hurricanes from Egypt arrived to protect the two ships. They were too late, of course, to do anything apart from protecting the recovery of the survivors. *Calcutta* sank in less than three minutes, taking 107 of her crew down with her.

The evacuation from Sphakia on the night of Saturday 31 May and Sunday 1 June was the last act of a brutal and hard-fought campaign. Allied troops were still left on Crete, including, to the Navy's deep regret, a contingent of Royal Marines, and many of the Australians who had been protecting the beachhead. Over 1,000 of them would eventually escape. Still, the decision had been made. General Wavell had already decided that the remainder of the Cretan garrison was to capitulate. By midday, Sphakia was in German hands, and the last opportunity to evacuate the remaining troops had gone. Cunningham, though, was justifiably proud of what his ships and men had achieved, and the fact that, regardless of the cost, they had not let the army down.

Shortly before the war, the vintage Ceres-class light cruiser *Coventry* was converted into an AA cruiser. While not as powerful as the modern Dido-class ships, they proved invaluable during the Crete campaign. On 1 June, *Coventry* had to rescue survivors from her sister ship *Calcutta*, after the latter was sunk off the Egyptian coast.

AFTERMATH

The naval battle for Crete had been extremely costly. The Royal Navy had lost three cruisers (*Calcutta, Gloucester* and *Fiji*) and six destroyers (*Greyhound, Hereward, Imperial, Juno, Kandahar* and *Kelly*), together with 1,828 men, while another 183 were wounded. Three battleships, an aircraft carrier, six cruisers and seven destroyers had also been damaged, some so severely that it would take several months or more before they were returned to service. The Mediterranean Fleet had been gravely weakened, and Cunningham now barely had sufficient ships at his disposal to maintain control of the eastern Mediterranean. Effectively, he was left with the battleship *Queen Elizabeth*, the light cruiser *Ajax* and the AA cruiser *Coventry* ready for immediate service, plus a handful of destroyers. However, all of their crews were completely exhausted, having been in action almost continually since mid-April.

The Luftwaffe had suffered, too, reporting the loss of 284 aircraft of various kinds, and another 125 damaged. Of these, around 170 were Ju 52 transport planes shot down or damaged beyond repair during the airborne invasion. Luftflotte VIII reported the loss of 118 fighters and bombers shot down, with another 21 written off due to damage, and 12 wrecked due to non-combat reasons. Afterwards, the Mediterranean Fleet claimed 22 confirmed kills, a further 11 probable kills and 22 aircraft damaged and driven off. The majority of these appear to have been Ju 87s from StG 2 and Ju 88s from LG 1. So, Richthofen's victory over the Royal Navy had not been a bloodless one. Altogether during the campaign, the Luftwaffe claimed to have lost 311 aircrew killed or missing, and another 127 wounded. The airborne invasion of Crete had also been extremely costly, and of the 22,000 men who took part, over 6,500 became casualties, with 3,774 of these either killed or posted missing. This total included the German mountain troops lost when the *Lupo* convoy was intercepted by Rear Admiral Glennie's Force D.

While the Crete campaign had been a disaster for the Allies, the evacuation had been a huge success. Of the 32,000 troops of the Crete garrison, approximately 4,000 Greek and Commonwealth troops had been killed, and another 4,000 captured before the evacuation began. Of the remaining 24,000 troops, the Mediterranean Fleet managed to rescue 16,500 of them. The remainder, apart from up to 1,000 who managed to escape by other means, were taken prisoner during the days following the official capitulation of the garrison. These prisoners included survivors from the destroyers *Greyhound* and *Imperial*, who had shipwrecked on Crete or the islands in the Kythera Strait. For Cunningham, the success of the evacuation,

The 2-pdr pom-pom was the standard close-range anti-aircraft weapon used on Commonwealth ships during 1941. This version, mounted on a British destroyer, is unusual, as in the fleet off Crete, most were multi-barrelled versions – the eight-barrelled pom-pom being the most common.

carried out against the advice of the Middle East's army and air force chiefs, was a vindication of his determination 'not to let the army down'. In his report on the campaign, Cunningham summed up the value of all this when he wrote:

> It is not easy to convey how heavy was the strain that men and ships sustained. Apart from the cumulative effect of prolonged seagoing over extended periods, it has to be remembered that in this last instance ships' companies had none of the inspiration of battle with the enemy to bear them up. Instead they had the unceasing anxiety of the task of trying to bring away in safety thousands of their own countrymen … they had started the evacuation already over-tired, and they had to carry it out under conditions of severe air attack such as had only recently caused grievous losses to the fleet. There is rightly little credit or glory to be expected in these operations of retreat, but I feel that the

Rear Admiral Edward King commanded the Mediterranean Fleet's 15th Cruiser Squadron, flying his flag in *Dido*. After the Crete campaign, Cunningham criticized him for his lack of aggression in pursuing the *Sagittario* convoy, but by breaking contact he probably saved the ships under his command. Although promoted afterwards, he never held another seagoing command.

spirit of tenacity shown by those who took part should not go unrecorded.

He went on to describe how close to breaking point the crews were by the end of this long and gruelling campaign. That they still uncomplainingly did their duty was a credit to them, and to the traditions of the Royal Navy. As Cunningham put it himself, the 300-year-old tradition had been maintained, even in the face of a most devastatingly effective display of modern air power. One of the best endorsements of his fleet's handling of the evacuation came from a New Zealand officer who was rescued first from Greece, and then from Crete. He said that he and his men had absolute faith that, if they could just reach the coast, the Navy would rescue them. They did, and the Navy were there. One man flashed SOS on his torch, and out to sea a warship replied, came in and took them off. Despite all it had been through, the fleet was there for them.

After Crete, Cunningham still had a naval campaign to fight, and to win. The loss of Crete had weakened the Mediterranean Fleet's hold on the eastern Mediterranean, as much of it now lay within range of Luftwaffe airfields in Libya and Crete. However, the Axis invasion of the Soviet Union changed the whole strategic situation, as the bulk of the German air armadas were moved north to support this immense operation. As Cunningham's warships were either repaired or replaced, he was able to re-establish sea control over the region, and to support operations designed to re-establish its presence in the central Mediterranean. After a brief naval campaign against the Vichy French in the waters off Lebanon, the focal point of the naval war shifted to Malta, and attempts to force convoys through to the beleaguered island from both Alexandria and Gibraltar. It also involved attacks on Axis supply routes between Italy and North Africa.

As a result, Crete and the Aegean became something of a backwater. Cunningham was fortunate in that throughout the Crete campaign, and in the months that followed, the Italian battle fleet never repeated its foray into the eastern Mediterranean that resulted in its defeat off Matapan. Instead, it concentrated its resources on protecting its own North African convoys, and opposing the Allied ones bound for Malta. In effect, despite all Cunningham's efforts, by the end of the Crete campaign the Mediterranean Fleet was 'on the ropes'. The Royal Navy's control of the seas through sea power had been negated by the Luftwaffe's air power. It would be another three years before the Allies had the military will or wherewithal to return to the Aegean. This demonstration of the effectiveness of air power, though, had no other long-term benefit to the Axis cause. Thanks to the commitment of the Axis powers to the Eastern Front, and the lack of aggression shown by the Regia Marina after Matapan, Cunningham's fleet was given time to recover. The admiral would make good use of this opportunity, and despite its setbacks, his fleet would soon go back onto the offensive once again.

THE BATTLEFIELD TODAY

Like any battle fought at sea, there is no site to visit, nor lasting monument marking where the naval struggle took place. Instead, the waters around Crete have become a haven for yachtsmen and holidaymakers, most of whom have no knowledge of the sacrifices made by both sides along these same beautiful coastlines. At least on Crete itself, visitors can gain an impression of the fighting there, and visit the battlefields and war graves which bear testimony to where the battle of Crete was fought. For those interested in the naval struggle, there is little to see, save for the modern appearance of Souda and Heraklion, now both popular cruise ship destinations, or Sphakia to the south, which at least has the benefit of being less developed than the other ports. In each of them, though, and armed with the knowledge of what went on there in May 1941, it is still possible to strip back the trappings of the intervening years, and imagine the scene there during the campaign.

As for the ships, they have all long gone, save for the wrecks, which are now officially war graves and therefore off limits to divers. However, for those who still want to step onto the deck of a wartime British cruiser or destroyer, then you can, by visiting HMS *Belfast* in the Pool of London opposite the Tower of London, or HMS *Cavalier* in Chatham Historic Dockyard. While *Belfast* never took part in the campaign, she is similar enough to HMS *Gloucester* to gain a good understanding of what she and *Fiji* looked like, both above and below decks. Similarly *Cavalier*, although a late-war destroyer design, is merely a slightly improved version of the J/K/N-class destroyers like *Juno*, *Kashmir* and *Kelly*, whose rusting remains still lie in the waters around Crete.

In terms of museums, The Battle for Crete and National Resistance Museum in Heraklion, opened in 1994, is an excellent interpretative centre, and while it primarily concentrates on the land battle, it touches on naval matters, particularly the evacuation. The Historical Museum of Crete, also in Heraklion, has a gallery covering the battle. In the United Kingdom the Royal Naval Museum in Portsmouth, the Imperial War Museum in south London, and the National Maritime Museum in Greenwich are all worth visiting for their relevant interpretive displays, ship models and collections of relevant photographs, ship plans and artwork. Similarly, the Luftwaffe Museum in Berlin-Gatow contains galleries which mention the campaign, and discuss the technical aspects of the aircraft involved.

For those eager to see these aircraft for themselves, there are two surviving Ju 87 'Stukas', in Chicago's Museum of Science and Industry, and in the Royal Air Force Museum in Hendon, north London. A third, in a private museum in Everett, WA, is currently being restored. The RAF Museum also has a Ju 88 in its collection, as does the National Museum of the United States Air Force in Dayton, OH. The RAF Museum also has an He III, as does the Royal Norwegian Air Force Museum in Gardermoen, Oslo's main airport, and at the Museo del Aire to the south of Madrid. Two surviving Italian SM.79 'Sparviero' bombers can be seen at the Italian Air Force Museum (Museo Storico Aeronautica Militare) in Bracciano 30 miles north-west of Rome, and in the Gianni Caproni Museum of Aeronautics (Museo dell'Aeronautica) in Trento, north-west Italy.

FURTHER READING

Beevor, Anthony, *Crete: The Battle and the Resistance* (London, 1991, John Murray Ltd)

Brescia, Maurizio, *Mussolini's Navy: A Reference Guide to the Regia Marina 1930–45* (Barnsley, 2012, Seaforth Publishing)

Campbell, John, *Naval Weapons of World War Two* (London, 1985, Conway Maritime Press)

Carruthers, Bob, *Stuka: Trumpets of Jericho* (Slough, 2012, Archive Media Publishing Ltd)

Clark, Alan, *The Fall of Crete* (London, 1991, Cassell & Co.)

Falconer, Jonathan, *Junkers Ju-87 Stuka: Owners' Workshop Manual* (Yeovil, 2018, Haynes Publishing)

Forty, George, *Battle for Crete* (Hersham, 2001, Ian Allen Ltd)

Friedman, Norman, *Naval Radar* (London, 1981, Harper Collins)

——, *British Destroyers, from Earliest Days to the Second World War* (Barnsley, 2009, Seaforth Publishing)

——, *British Cruisers: Two World Wars and After* (Barnsley, 2010, Seaforth Publishing)

——, *Naval Firepower: Battleship Guns and Gunnery in the Dreadnought Era* (Barnsley, 2013, Seaforth Publishing)

Gardiner, Robert (ed.), *Conway's All the World's Fighting Ships, 1922–1946* (London, 1980, Conway Maritime Press)

Greene, Jack and Massignani, Alessandro, *The Naval War in the Mediterranean 1940–43* (Rochester, 1998, Chatham Publishing)

Grove, Eric, *Sea Battles in Close-Up*, 2 vols (Shepperton, 1988/1993, Ian Allen Ltd)

Heathcote, Tony, *The British Admirals of the Fleet 1734–1995* (Barnsley, 2002, Pen & Sword)

Lavery, Brian, *Churchill's Navy: The Ships, Men and Organisation 1939–45* (London, 2006, Conway)

Ministry of Information, *The Mediterranean Fleet: Greece to Tripoli – The Admiralty Account of Naval Operations, April 1941 to January 1943* (London, 1944, HMSO)

Morris, Douglas, *Cruisers of the Royal and Commonwealth Navies* (Liskeard, 1987, Maritime Books)

O'Hara, Vincent, *Struggle for the Middle Sea: The Great Navies at War in the Mediterranean 1940–45* (London, 2009, Conway Maritime Press)

Pack, S.W.C., *The Battle for Crete* (Shepperton, 1973, Ian Allen Ltd)

Preston, Anthony (ed.), *Jane's Fighting Ships of World War II* (London, 1989, Bracken Books; originally published London, 1947, Jane's Publishing Company)

Price, Alfred, *The Luftwaffe Data Book* (London, 1997, Greenhill Books)

Roberts, John, *British Warships of the Second World War* (Barnsley, 2017, Seaforth Publishing)

Roskill, Stephen W., *The War at Sea*, Vol. 1: History of the Second World War series (London 1954, HM Stationery Office)

Smith, J.R., Kay, Anthony and Creek, E.J., *German Aircraft of the Second World War* (London, 1972, Putnam)

Tarrant, V.E., *Battleship Warspite* (London, 1990, Arms & Armour Press)

Thomas, David A., *Crete 1941: The Battle at Sea* (London, 1972, André Deutsch Ltd)

Ward, John, *Hitler's Stuka Squadrons: The Ju 87 at War, 1939–45* (Cheltenham, 2004, The History Press)

Whitley, M.J., *Cruisers of World War Two: An International Encyclopaedia* (London, 1995, Arms & Armour Press)

——, *Destroyers of World War Two: An International Encyclopaedia* (London, 1998, Arms & Armour Press)

Winton, John, *Cunningham: The Greatest Admiral since Nelson* (London, 1998, John Murray Ltd)

INDEX

Figures in **bold** refer to illustrations, captions and plates.

AA capability 18–19, 41, 43, 51, 57, 58, 59, 60
AA watch 20
air superiority 5, **5**, 16, 26, 75, 79, 92
air support 19, 40, 87, 88
air transport 22, 37
aircraft 19–20, 23, 46, 50
    Bristol Blenheim (UK) 19, 34
    DFS glider (Germany) 22, **37**
    Dornier Do 17 (Germany) **23**, 50, 51, 57
    Fairey Fulmar (UK) 20, **76**, 77, 83
    Hawker Hurricane (UK) 19–20, 83, 89
    Heinkel He 111 (Germany) 43, 50, 77, 87, 93
    Junkers Ju 52 (Germany) 22, **25**, **40**, 46
    Junkers Ju 87 Stuka dive-bomber (Germany) 8, 23, **23**, **27**, 28, 30, 33, 34, 40, 43, 50, 56–57, 60, 61, **70–71** (72), **73**, 73, 77, **80–81**, 82, **84–85** (86), 87, 93
    Junkers Ju 88 (Germany) **23**, 24, 30, 43, 50, 51, 56–57, 67, 73, 77, 79, **80–81**, 83, 87, 88–89, 90, 93
    Messerschmitt Me 109 (Germany) 50, **58**, 59, 67
    SM.79 (Italy) 34, 38, 41, **81**, 93
    SM.84 (Italy) 38, 41, **81**
    Z.10007bis 'Alcione' (Italy) 41, **81**
Allied retreat in the Balkans 5
Allison, Cmdr John 48
ammunition supplies 18–19, 29, 31, 43, 51, 55, 56, 57, 60, 61, **64**, 65, 67
Arliss, Capt Stephen 79, 87, **88**
Auchinleck, Gen Claude 14

Back, Capt Geoffrey 83, **83**
Baillie-Grohman, Rear-Adm Tom 14, 29, 30
battle fatigue 29, 56, 90, 91
Battle of Britain 16
Battle of Calabria (Punta Stilo), the 7
Battle of Cape Matapan, the 5, 8, 9, 14, 17, 18, 25, 30, 92
Battle of Cape Spartivento (Teulada), the 7
Biggs, Cmdr Hilary **69**
'Black Thursday' (22 May 1941) **11**, **56**, 56–68, **58**, **60**, 62–63, **64**, 65, **70–71** (72)
Bowyer-Smith, Capt Philip 87
British Army, the 25–26, 91
    2nd New Zealand Division 21
British control of the Mediterranean 5, 9, 90, 92
British naval bases 6
British strategy 5–6, 7–8, 10, 11–12, **18**, 24, **25**, 25–27, 32–33, 35, 37–38, **38**, 40, 46, 49, 51–56, 57, **58**, 60, 68, 75, 76, 77–79, 90–92
Brown, Lt-Cmdr Cecil 82
Brownrigg, Cmdr Thomas 77–79

chains of command 60
chronology of events 11–12
Churchill, Winston 5, 8, 10, 14, 15, 31, 55, 79, **79**
Clark, Cmdr Max 88
convoy routes 7, 23, 28, 31, 92
cruisers
    Dido-class AA cruisers 26, **80**, 89
    Leander-class 18, **32**, **46**, 80
    Town-class 57
Cunningham, Adm Andrew B. 5, **5**, 6, 7, 9, 10, 12, **13**, 13–14, 15, 18, 19, **25**, 25–26, 27, 29, 32, 33, 35, **35**, 37, 38, 40, 46, 49, 51, 55, 57, 68, 73, 74, 75, 76, 77, **82**, 83, 89, 90–92, **92**

damage 6, 7, 11, 12, 17, 34, 41, 43, **46**, 47, 48, **49**, 51, 55, 57, **57**, 58, 59–60, 61–64, 65, 73, 77, 79, **80**, 82, 87, **87**, 88, **88**, 89, 90
de Winton Kitcat, Lt-Cmdr Charles 82
destroyers
    D/E-class **35**, 80
    G/H/I-class 56, **69**, 80, 82
    J/K/N class 18, **20**, 33, 43, 48, 50, **69**, 79, 80, 88, 93
Dinort, Oberst Oskar 27, 28, 50
dive-bombers 16, 48

evacuations from Greece and Crete 6, 7, 9, 10, 12, 13, 15, **19**, 21, 29–31, **69**, 78, 79–82, **80–81**, **82**, 87–89, **89**, 90–92

Fisher, Capt Douglas 58, 59
Förset, Vice-Adm 28
Freyberg, Maj-Gen Bernard 14–15, 20, 21, 30, 32
fuel supplies 11, 27, 28, 31, 33, 35, 41, 50, 56, **59**, 67, 74, 75, 76, 80
Fulgosi, Lieutenant Giuseppe 49, 51, **54**, 55

Geisler, General Hans 8
George II, King **69**, 73
German Heer, the
    Afrikakorps 8–9
    5.Gebirgs-Division 22, 23, 27, 40, 46, 47, 48, 51, 55, 90
German invasion of Crete 5–6, 10, **25**, 26, 27, 32–37, **34**, 36
German invasion of the Balkans 8, 9, 10
German strategy 5, 6, 8–9, 10, 11, 16, 22, 23, 27–28, 31, 37, 40–41, 46, 47, 49–50, 56, 57–58, 92
Glennie, Rear-Adm Irvine 11, 12, 14, 22, 26, 33, 35, **38**, 41, **44**, 46, 47, 48, 49, 50, 57, 90
GOC (General Officer Commanding), the 14
Grantham, Capt Guy 89
Greek army and strategy 8, 10

HACS (High-Angle Control System), the 18, 19, **20**, 26, **32**, 33, 57, 61
Hampton, Capt Thomas 58
Heraklion 11, 32, 33, 34, 37, 40, 83
Hitler, Adolf 8, 10, 27
Hitschhold, Staffelkapitän Hubertus 73

Iachino, Admiral Angelo 9
intelligence 26, 31–32, 33, 34, 37, 51
Italian declarations of war 6
Italian invasions of Egypt and Greece 7–8
Italian strategy 7, 24, **49**, 92

Kasos Strait, the 35, 37, 38, **39**, 40, 41, 46, **46**, 51, 55, 75, 79
    attack on Force B **80–81**, 82–83, **84–85** (86)
King, Rear-Adm Edward 11, 14, 21, 26, 33, 35, 38, 40, 46–47, 49, 51, **51**, **54**, 55, 57, 58, 60, 61, 65, 68, 69, **72**, 74, 87, **92**
Kriegsmarine, the 23, 28
    Bismarck (battleship) 76
    1st Motor-Sailing Flotilla **44–45**, 47, 48, 49
    2nd Motor-Sailing Flotilla 51
Kythera Strait, the 37, **42**, 43, 47, 48, 50, 55, 57, 58, 68

Langmaid, Lt-Cmdr Rowland 41, 64
Lee-Barber, Lt-Cmdr John 56
Löhr, General der Flieger Alexander 16
Longmore, Air Chief Marshal Sir Arthur 15, 29, 32

losses 6, 7, 10, 11, 12, 18, **19**, 30–31, 41, **44**, 46, 48, 58, 59, **60**, 61–64, 67, 68, 70–71(72), 73–75, 77, 80, 83, **83**, 89, 90
Luftwaffe, the 5, 6, 10, 11, 15, 16, 23, 24, 27, 30, 33, **34**, 47, 55, 57, 58, **60**, 79, 92
    Divisions
        7.Flieger-Division 22
        22.Luftlande-Division 22, 27
    Fallschirmjäger (paratroopers) 16, **16**, **25**, 27, 37, **37**
    Fliegerkorps 16
        VIII.Fliegerkorps 15, **15**, 16, 23, **23**, 24, 26, 27–28, 33–34, 37, 49, 59, **62**, 68, **69**
        X.Fliegerkorps 8, 77
        XI.Fliegerkorps 16, 22, 23
    Gruppen 50
        I./LG 1 51, 57
        I./StG 2 **70–71**(72), 73
        II./JG 77 67
        II./StG 2 77
        III./JG 77 50, 59
        III./LG 1 77, **81**, 89
        III./StG 2 **80–81**, **84–85** (86)
    Jadgeschwader (JG)
        JG 77 23, 24, 50
    Kampfgeschwader (KG)
        KG 2 23, **23**, 24, 50, 51, 57, 65
    Lehrgeschwader (LG)
        LG 1 23, 24, 50, 56–57, 73, 77, 79, **80–81**, 83, 87, 90
        LG 2 65, 67
    Sturzkampfgeschwader (StG) 28
        StG 1 23, 24
        StG 2 23, 24, **27**, 28, 50, 56–57, 60, **80–81**, 82, 87, 90
        StG 3 23, 24
        StG 77 24
    Zerstörergeschwader (ZG)
        ZG 26 23, 24, 50
Luftwaffe Museum, Berlin, the 93
Lumley, Petty Officer 43
Lupo convoy action (21 May 1941) **44–45**, 46, 47–48, 51, 90

Mack, Capt Philip 22, 37, 40, **43**, 47, 73, 88
Madden, Lt-Cmdr Charles 59
Maleme airfield 11, 12, 20, 32, 34, 35, 46
Malta naval base 6–7
manoeuvreability 48, **60**, 67, **72**, 73
map of strategic situation (April–June 1941) **4**
Marshall-A'Deane, Cmdr Walter 60, 68
MAS torpedo boats (Italy) 11, **38**, 38–40, 41, **49**
McCall, Capt Henry **87**
McCarthy, Capt Desmond 75, 76
merchant shipping attacks 34
Metaxas Line, the 10
military strength and complements 17, 18, 20–21, 22–23, 24, 35, 50, 90
Mimbelli, Capitano di Corvetta Francesco 28, **44**, 47, 48
Morasutti, Lieutenant Mario 41, 43
Morgan, Capt Charles 65
Mountbatten, Capt Lord Louis 46–47, 65, 68, 69, **72**, 73
Munn, Lt-Cmdr William 82, 83
museums and modern exhibits 93
Mussolini, Benito 6, 8

naval search formations 51
New Zealand Expeditionary Force, the 14–15
night operations 24, 30, 32, 34, 35, 37, 43, 46, 74
North African theater, the **4**, 5, 7–9, 14, 31

OKW (Oberkommando der Wehrmacht), the 27
open bridge arrangement **48, 57**
operations 14, 31
  Barbarossa (June 1941) 27, 92
  Demon (April 1941) 29–31
  Lustre (March 1941) 8, 9
  Maritsa (April 1941) 10, 22
  Merkur (May–June 1941) 10, 27, 33
  Tiger (April 1941) 26, 31, 32
Operations Room, the **22**
operations west of Crete (22–23 May 191) **66**, 68–69
orders of battle 21–22, 24

Pleydell-Bouverie, Capt the Hon. Edward 74
Plotting Officer, the **22**
Pound, Adm Dudley 13
POWs 90
Pridham-Wippell, Vice-Adm Sir Henry 11, 12, 14, **14**, 21, 26, 29, 33, 76

Queen Elizabeth-class battleships 17, **18**

RAF, the 5, 10, 15, 83, 87, 88
  squadrons 19, 20, 46
    30 Sqn 19, 34
    203 Sqn 19, 34
RAN (Royal Australian Navy), the 18
  HMAS *Napier* (destroyer) 12, 18, 35, 79, 87
  HMAS *Nizam* (destroyer) 12, 37, 47, 73, 79, 87, **88**
  HMAS *Perth* (cruiser) 9, 12, 18, 27, 35, 38, 51, **54**, 55, 58, 87
ranges 23, **23**, 24, 55
Ravenhill, Cmdr 77
Rawlings, Rear-Adm Bernard 11, **11**, 14, 21, 27, 33, 35, 40, 43, 46, 49, 57, **58**, 60, 61, 73, 74, 79–82, **80**, 83, **83**
reconnaissance **23**, 28, 38, 40, 46, 50, 51, 55, 88
Regia Aeronautica, the 7, 23, 41, 43
  50 Gruppo 41, **81**
  92 Gruppo 41, **81**
Regia Marina, the 5, 6, 7, **8**, 9, 23, 30, 33, 92
  MAS Flotillas 38–40, 83
  ships and torpedo boats
    Pola (cruiser) 9, **30**
    RM *Lupo* (torpedo boat) 24, **28**, **44–45**, 47–48, 60, 90
    RM *Sagittario* (torpedo boat) 24, **49**, 50, 51–55, **52–53 (54)**
    Vittorio Veneto (battleship) 9
  Supermarina 23–24
reinforcements 17, 22, 28, 31, 46–47, 75, 76, 77
repairs 17, 92
rescue missions 41–43, 48, 50, 60, 61, 68, **68**, 74, 83, **89**, 90
Richthofen, General der Flieger Baron Wolfram von **15**, 15–16, 23, 27, 28, 34, 40, 49, 50, 77
Richthofen, Manfred von ('The Red Baron') 15, **15**, 16
Robson, Cmdr William 68
Rommel, General Erwin 5, 8–9, 31
Rowley, Capt Henry 21, 26, 33, 46, 49, 56, 57, **60**, 61–64
Royal Marines, the 32, 68, 79, 89
Royal Navy, the 5–6, **8**, **20**, 22, 25–26, 28
  forces
    A 11, 12, 21, 26, 27, 35, 49, 76–77
    A1 11, 21, 27, 33, 35, 37, 43, 46, 49, 57, 58, 60, **63**, 65, 69, 73
    B 11, 12, 21, 26, 27, 33, 35, 37, 40, 43, 49, **56**, 56–57, 60, **63**, 79–83, **80–81**, **84–85 (86)**

C 11, 12, 21, 26, 33, 34, 35, 37, 38–40, 41–43, 46, 49, **50**, 51–56, **52–53 (54)**, 57, 61, **63**, 65, 79, 87–89, **88**
D 11, 12, 21, 26–27, 33, 35, 37, **38**, 40, **41**, 43, **44–45**, 46–48, 49, **49**, 57, 87, 88, **89**, 90
E (14th Destroyer Flotilla) 22, 37, 40, **43**, 47, 73, **88**
5th Destroyer Flotilla 46–47, **69**, **70–71 (72)**, 73
10th Destroyer Flotilla 47, 69
15th Destroyer Flotilla 65, 68
Mediterranean Fleet 6, 13, 14, **14**, 16, **25**, 27, **27**, 32, 49, 90, 92
MNBDO (Mobile Naval Base Defence Organization) 32
ships 30, 34, 35, 73, 87
  HMS *Abdiel* (minelayer) 12, **74**, 75, 76, 77
  HMS *Ajax* (cruiser) 7, 12, 18, 27, 35, **41**, **44–45**, 47, 48, 57, 75, 79, 80, 82, 90
  HMS *Barham* (battleship) 12, 17, **18**, 26, 76, 77
  HMS *Calcutta* (cruiser) 12, 18, 37, 40, 41, 51, 58, 87, 88–89, **89**, 90
  HMS *Carlisle* (cruiser) 11, 18, 19, 37, 51, 55, 58
  HMS *Coventry* (cruiser) 18, 26, 34, 69, 88–89, **89**, 90
  HMS *Decoy* (destroyer) 35, 73, 74, 79, **80**
  HMS *Defender* (destroyer) 19, 68, 73, 74, 75, 87
  HMS *Diamond* (destroyer) 10, 30
  HMS *Dido* (cruiser) 12, 18, 19, 26, **26**, 35, **41**, **44–45**, 47, 57, 75, 79, 80, 82, 83, **84–85 (86)**, 87, 92
  HMS *Fiji* (cruiser) 11, 18, 26, 31, 32, 35, 46, 56, 57, 60, 61, 64, **64**, 65–67, 68, 69, 74, 90
  HMS *Formidable* (carrier) 9, 12, 17, 28, 33, **75**, **76**, 76–77
  HMS *Glenroy* (Landing Ship) 69, 76
  HMS *Gloucester* (cruiser) 11, 18, 26, 32, 35, 46, **50**, 57, 57, 60, **60**, 61–64, 90, 93
  HMS *Greyhound* (destroyer) 11, 18, 35, 46, 56, 60–61, 68, 74, 90
  HMS *Griffin* (destroyer) 35, 46, 56, **56**
  HMS *Hasty* (destroyer) 35, **44–45**, 57, 87
  HMS *Hereward* (destroyer) 35, **44–45**, 57, 79, **80**, 82, 82–83, 90
  HMS *Hero* (destroyer) 12, 18, 35, **69**, 73, 74
  HMS *Hotspur* (destroyer) 31, 35, 75, 79, **80**, 82
  HMS *Ilex* (destroyer) 37, 47, 73
  HMS *Illustrious* (carrier) 7, 8, 10, 17
  HMS *Imperial* (destroyer) 35, 75, 79, 82, 90
  HMS *Jackal* (destroyer) 47, 65, 68, 73, 79, **80**, **84–85 (86)**
  HMS *Jaguar* (destroyer) 68, 73, 74, 75, 87
  HMS *Janus* (destroyer) 35, **44–45**, 47, 57, 87
  HMS *Jervis* (destroyer) 37, **43**, 47, 73, 87
  HMS *Juno* (destroyer) 11, 18, 35, 38, 41, 43, 58, 90, 93
  HMS *Kandahar* (destroyer) 35, 38, 41, 43, 58, 60, 61, 64, 65, 67–68, 69, 74, 79, 87, 90
  HMS *Kashmir* (destroyer) 11, 47, 65, 68, **68** 70–71 **(72)**, 73–74, 93
  HMS *Kelly* (destroyer) 11, 18, 47, 48, 65, 68, **68**, **69**`, 70–71 **(72)**, 74, 90, 93

HMS *Kelvin* (destroyer) 47, 65, 73, 79, 87
HMS *Kimberley* (destroyer) 35, **44–45**, 57, 75, 79, **79**, 80
HMS *Kingston* (destroyer) 35, 38, 41, **50**, **52–53 (54)**, 55, 58, 64, 67–68, 69, 74
HMS *Kipling* (destroyer) 59, 60, 61, 65, 68, **68**, **70–71 (72)**, 73, 74, 75
HMS *Naiad* (cruiser) 11, 18, 19, 26, **26**, 31, 35, 38, 51, **51**, **52–53 (54)**, 55, 57, 58, 60, 61
HMS *Nubian* (destroyer) 12, 18, **33**, 35, 38, 41, **52–53 (54)**, 58, 77
HMS *Orion* (cruiser) 12, 18, **32**, 35, 41, **44–45**, 46, 47, 48, 57, 79, 80, 83, **83**, **84–85 (86)**
HMS *Phoebe* (cruiser) 18, 19, 26, **26**, 27, 34, 87, **89**
HMS *Queen Elizabeth* (battleship) 14, 17, 18, 26, 31, 76, 90
HMS *Stuart* (destroyer) 47, 69, 87
HMS *Valiant* (battleship) 11, 17, **18**, 27, 33, 35, 58, 60, 65
HMS *Vendetta* (destroyer) 47, 69
HMS *Voyager* (destroyer) 47, 69
HMS *Warspite* (battleship) 11, 13, 17, **18**, 27, 33, 35, **35**, 58, 58, 59–60, 61, 77
HMS *Wryneck* (destroyer) 10, 30
HMS *York* (cruiser) 34, **34**, **38**
squadrons **11**
  15th Cruiser 18, **92**

Sagitario action (22 May 1941) **50**, 51–55, **52–53 (54)**, 92
Scarpanto airfield **43**, 76, 88
Schuster, Adm Karlgeorg 23, 24, 46, 47, 51
sea denial 28
Sephton, Petty Officer Alfred 34
ship wrecks as war graves 93
Sicilian Narrows, the 8, 25, 28
Somerville, Lt-Cmdr Philip **50**, 55
Somerville, Vice-Adm James 31
SS *Lossiemouth* 34
St Clair-Ford, Lt-Cmdr Aubry 59, 74
steel hull protection **49**
Student, General der Flieger Kurt **16**, 16–17, 22, 23, 46, 49
Suda Bay 11, 23, 29, 32, 34, **34**, 35, 38, 68, 74, 75
supply problems and logistics 27, 32, 75
surface search radar 47

Tedder, Air Marshal Arthur 15, 77
'Tiger convoy,' the 17, 18, 31
topography of Crete 32
Tothill, Cmdr John 47
Type 279 radar 38
Tyrwhitt, Cmdr John 38, 41

Ultra intelligence reports 26, 32, 33

Walker, Leading Seaman Clem 67
Waller, Capt Hector 47, 69, 73, 74, 87
Wavell, Gen Archibald 7, 8, 12, 14, 26, 29, 31, 32, 77, 79, 89
weaponry 19, **20, 26**, 41, **41**
  SC250 bomb (Germany) **23**, 67, 73–74, 77, **84–85 (86)**, 87, **87**, 89
  0.5in. machine gun (UK) 19, **19**
  2-pdr pom-pom (UK) 19, **20**, 64, **91**
  4in. HA AA gun (UK) 32, 59
  4.7in./45 Mark XII QF gun (UK) **33**, 55
  20mm Oerlikon gun (UK) **20**, 74
William-Powlett, Capt Peveril 64, 65–67, 68
Wilson, Gen Maitland 29
World War I 13, 14, 15–16